T0326560

Advance Praise for *The Labyrinth of Sustainability*

"This excellent book shows that there are companies in Latin America taking seriously their social duty towards sustainability—with positive business results. This book should also be viewed as a call to action for the many others still lagging behind."

—Ernesto Zedillo, Director, Yale Center for the Study of Globalization, and Former President of Mexico

"Never before has it been so important to change the conversation about how corporate leaders can step up to the challenge of creating a sustainable future. *The Labyrinth of Sustainability* profiles real success stories in Latin America that show what is possible and why every business leader should pay attention."

—Jaime Serra Puche, Chairman, SAI Law and Economics, and Former Minister of Trade, Mexico

"*The Labyrinth of Sustainability* offers a roadmap to corporate best practice in Latin America, highlighting the experience of real companies and illustrating that sustainable practices can be good for business. It is not a theoretical treatise, but a compilation of successful business strategies that demonstrate what is possible in terms of both competitiveness and sustainability."

—Carlos Pascual, Senior Vice President, Global Energy, IHS Markit, and Former US Ambassador to Mexico

"An enlightening, in-depth analysis of how sustainability has moved from the last page of the annual report to the front and center of corporate strategy in Latin America."

—Christiana Figueres, Convenor, Mission 2020, and Former Executive Secretary, UN Framework Convention on Climate Change

"Sustainability has evolved from being about corporate social responsibility to a great investment opportunity for private sector firms in Latin America."

—Juan Pablo Bonilla, Manager, Climate Change and Sustainable Development Sector, Inter-American Development Bank

"The way that business approaches sustainability is changing rapidly as new opportunities and challenges emerge. The picture has become more complex—it's no longer just about emissions, reputation, or jobs. Rather, it's about all these aspects at the same time. *The Labyrinth of Sustainability* examples show that smart companies have now integrated sustainability deeply into their decision-making process and are proving that they can be more successful by considering not just the financial return, but also their impact on society and the environment."

—Peter Bakker, President and CEO, World Business Council for Sustainable Development

"An inspiring book for Latin American corporations demonstrating the importance of companies going beyond social responsibility to being true corporate citizens who positively impact and influence the communities and the environment in which they live and work."

—Juan Fernando Posada, President, Latin America Selling & Market Operations, Procter & Gamble

"A pathbreaking book that arms readers with actionable insights based on real-world business experience. Invaluable for corporate practitioners and students alike."

—P. J. Simmons, Chairman, Corporate Eco Forum

"In *The Labyrinth of Sustainability*, Daniel Esty has compiled an impressive array of case studies on practical environmental sustainability actions taken by a wide range of companies across sectors and countries in Latin America. These examples serve as a beacon to a more sustainable future for Latin America."

—Richard Wells, President, The Lexington Group

The Labyrinth of Sustainability

ANTHEM ENVIRONMENT AND SUSTAINABILITY INITIATIVE

The *Anthem Environment and Sustainability Initiative (AESI)* seeks to push the frontiers of scholarship while simultaneously offering prescriptive and programmatic advice to policymakers and practitioners around the world. The programme publishes research monographs, professional and major reference works, upper-level textbooks and general interest titles. Professor Lawrence Susskind, as General Editor of AESI, oversees the below book series, each with its own series editor and an editorial board featuring scholars, practitioners and business experts keen to link theory and practice.

Anthem Strategies for Sustainable Development Series
Series Editor: Professor Lawrence Susskind (MIT)

Anthem Climate Change and Policy Series
Series Editor: Dr. Brooke Hemming (US EPA)

Anthem Diplomacy at the Food-Water-Energy Nexus Series
Series Editor: Professor Shafiqul Islam (Tufts University)

Anthem International Environmental Policy Series
Series Editor: Professor Saleem Ali (University of Delaware)

Anthem Big Data and Sustainable Cities Series
Series Editor: Sarah Williams (MIT)

Included within the AESI is the *Anthem EnviroExperts Review*. Through this online micro-review site, Anthem Press seeks to build a community of practice involving scientists, policy analysts and activists committed to creating a clearer and deeper understanding of how ecological systems – at every level – operate, and how they have been damaged by unsustainable development. This site publishes short reviews of important books or reports in the environmental field, broadly defined. Visit the site: www.anthemenviroexperts.com.

The Labyrinth of Sustainability

Green Business Lessons from Latin American Corporate Leaders

Edited by
Daniel C. Esty

ANTHEM PRESS

Anthem Press
An imprint of Wimbledon Publishing Company
www.anthempress.com

This edition first published in UK and USA 2019
by ANTHEM PRESS
75–76 Blackfriars Road, London SE1 8HA, UK
or PO Box 9779, London SW19 7ZG, UK
and
244 Madison Ave #116, New York, NY 10016, USA

British Library Cataloguing-in-Publication Data
A catalogue record for this book is available from the British Library.

ISBN-13: 978-1-78308-912-3 (Hbk)
ISBN-10: 1-78308-912-1 (Hbk)

ISBN-13: 978-1-78308-913-0 (Pbk)
ISBN-10: 1-78308-913-X (Pbk)

This title is also available as an e-book.

To Charles W. Cole, president of Amherst College (1946–61) and US ambassador to Chile (1961–63), who instilled in the editor his commitment to academic excellence, appreciation of the environment, and recognition of the importance of Latin America as a vital region facing significant challenges but with extraordinary resources, both human and natural.

CONTENTS

ILLUSTRATIONS

Figures

Tables

ACKNOWLEDGMENTS

This book would not have come together without extraordinary efforts on the part of many people and several institutions. At the outset I need to thank Isabel Studer Noguez (now the director of strategic partnerships at The Nature Conservancy in Mexico), who first highlighted for me the need for more scholarly exploration of corporate sustainability in Latin America and arranged for me to join her at the Global Institute for Sustainability at the Tecnológico de Monterrey's business school, the Escuela de Graduados en Administración y Dirección de Empresas (EGADE), in Mexico City as a Visiting STAR professor. Many of the chapters of this book emerged from our multiple years of collaboration and joint research on corporate sustainability in Mexico and beyond. Although Isabel left EGADE for a position in the Mexican government before this book came together, her influence through her students and thought leadership on corporate sustainability can be found on every page.

I am especially grateful for the financial support from the F.K. Weyerhaeuser Memorial Fund administered by the Center for Business and the Environment at Yale (cbey.yale.edu). The fund allowed us to cover travel costs and expenses for the research teams and host an April 2016 workshop at the Yale School of Management to review the draft book chapters and discuss the critical topics that the book covers. Jaan Elias, director of Case Study Research and Development at the Yale School of Management, provided engagement and guidance in support of the workshop. Brad Gentry and Stuart DeCew deserve special thanks for their enthusiasm and support of the Latin America Corporate Sustainability Analysis (LACSA) Project at Yale that undergirded the efforts that led to this book.

Additional financial support was provided by EGADE and thanks in this regard go to then EGADE Dean Dr. Maria de Lourdes Dieck Assad and National Associate Dean of Research Teo Ozuno. At Yale, three schools and three deans provided support that allowed the LACSA research initiative to come together as a book: Dean Indy Burke of the Yale School of Forestry and Environmental Studies, Dean Ted Snyder of the Yale School of Management, and Dean Heather Gerken of the Yale Law School.

Further recognition must be given to Dean Snyder for setting up the Global Network for Advanced Management (GNAM), which brings together 30 leading business schools across the world in a range of shared academic pursuits. Several of the Latin American participants in GNAM contributed to the research that has now emerged as *The Labyrinth of Sustainability*. Additional thanks go to INCAE Business School in Costa Rica (and Nicaragua) as well as FGV Escola de Administração de Empresas de São Paolo in Brazil for their partnership on this project.

At the Yale Center for Environmental Law and Policy (www.yale. edu/envirocenter), which hosted the LACSA initiative over three years, a number of people contributed to getting this book into its final form. This list includes YCELP Program Manager Tim Mason, former Associate Director Lisa Dale, and Chris Lewis, who took the laboring oar on editing the draft chapters. Matthew Archer, Sam Faries, Lucy Kessler, Laura Brush, Elizabeth Ruben, Claira Janover, Maggie Ferrato, Robert Little, Jonathan Silverthorne, and Hannah Abelow also contributed to the effort to bring the chapters together. We are also grateful for the editorial support of Alan Bisbort.

I am deeply appreciative of our publishing partnership with Anthem Press and its publisher and managing director, Tej P. S. Sood—as well as the Anthem teams in London and New York.

Finally, I want to thank all of the chapter authors—Mariana Cesín Sastré, Martha Sofia Cifuentes, Roger Nion Conaway, Santiago Cortés Villota, Isidro Marco A. Cristobal-Vazquez, Milagros De Camps Germán, Mariel Ferro Rivas, Aideé Figueroa López, Edwin Garcia, Margarita Heredia Soto, Siegfried King, Fairuz O. Loutfi Olivares,

Felipe Perez, Hellen Quinonez, and Francisco Gabriel Rodríguez González—who worked with us to dig out the often-hidden story of how companies across Latin America have begun to fold sustainability into their corporate strategies. I am grateful for the depth of research, scholarly care, and academic honesty that comes through in every chapter.

Daniel C. Esty
New Haven, Connecticut
January 2019

CONTRIBUTORS

Mariana Cesín Sastré is a PhD student in business administration at the EGADE Business School within the Tecnológico de Monterrey (Mexico City). She has worked on sustainable development at the Universidad Iberoamericana and in the hospitality industry. She obtained a bachelor's degree in international relations from Universidad Iberoamericana in Mexico City and an MSc in environmental policy and management from the University of Bristol (England).

Martha Sofia Cifuentes is a credit officer at Banco ProCredit in Managua, Nicaragua. She has worked for several global think tanks, including the Woodrow Wilson International Center for Scholars in Washington, DC, the Centro de Investigación y Desarrollo de la Educación in Santiago, Chile, and INCAE Business School where she was a senior researcher. She graduated from Georgetown University with an MA in Latin American studies (with a concentration in government) and a BA in government and history. Her research interests center on education, energy, political economy, sustainability, and international trade. She has authored several case studies and teaching notes on competitiveness, corporate governance, corporate social responsibility, ethics, and entrepreneurship.

Roger Nion Conaway serves as professor emeritus in management in the Soules College of Business at the University of Texas at Tyler. He previously worked as a professor in the School of Business at the Monterrey Institute of Technology (ITESM) in San Luis Potosí, Mexico, and at EGADE Business School in Monterrey. Dr. Conaway's industry experience includes work with FEMSA, ABB, Valeo, World Trade Center, ContiTec, and Cinépolis movie theatres. He has taught internationally in India, at the Central University of Haryana, the Florence University of the Arts, and through Steinbeis University's online program. He has coauthored five books, including *Principles of Responsible Management: Global Sustainability, Responsibility, and Ethics*, the first official textbook for the United Nations Principles for Responsible Management Education Academic Network.

Santiago Cortés Villota is the ESG manager at Amerra Capital Management, an asset management firm that provides strategic capital to upstream and midstream agri-business companies in the Americas and Western Europe. Santiago holds undergraduate degrees in industrial and environmental engineering from the Universidad de los Andes in Colombia and has over five years of experience in energy and sustainability consulting. He graduated with a master of environmental management degree from the Yale School of Forestry and Environmental Studies. His academic work has focused on innovative financial instruments. He supported the Colombian Delegation at the 2016 United Nations Conference of the Parties global climate change negotiations (COP 22), with a particular focus on climate finance issues. He has also conducted research for the Natural Infrastructure for Water team at the World Resources Institute.

Isidro Marco A. Cristobal-Vazquez is a management science doctoral candidate at Tecnológico de Monterrey's EGADE Business School, and he lectures at the Instituto Politecnico Nacional in Mexico City. He previously worked in the technology and logistics sectors. He holds a master of science degree in industrial engineering from Texas A&M University. His research focuses on innovation management and individual innovative behavior.

Milagros De Camps Germán is a legal consultant at the Green Climate Fund, a fund established within the United Nations Framework Convention on Climate Change to assist developing countries in adaptation to and mitigation of climate change. She was previously a Yale Fox International Fellow at the National University of Singapore, where she conducted research on energy security, climate change, and sustainable development in small island developing states. Milagros has also practiced corporate and energy law in the Dominican Republic, worked as a professor of corporate law, and cofounded the Dominican Business Council for Sustainable Development. She received her master of environmental management degree from the Yale School of Forestry and Environmental Studies, which she attended as a Fulbright scholar. She holds a JD from the Pontificia Universidad Católica Madre y Maestra in the Dominican Republic and an LLM from Boston University.

Daniel C. Esty is the Hillhouse Professor at Yale University with primary appointments in Yale's Environment and Law Schools and a secondary appointment at the Yale School of Management. He serves as director of the Yale Center for Environmental Law and Policy (www.yale.edu/envirocenter) and is on the Advisory Board of the Yale Center for Business and Environment (cbey.yale.edu), which he founded in 2006. Professor Esty is the author or editor of ten books and dozens of articles on environmental protection, energy, and sustainability—and their connections to policy, corporate strategy, competitiveness, trade, performance measurement, and economic success. His highly regarded prior study, *Green to Gold: How Smart Companies Use Environmental Strategy to Innovate, Create Value, and Build Competitive Advantage*, has recently been named the top-selling "green business" book of the past decade. Prior to taking up his Yale professorship in 1994, he served in a variety of senior positions at the US Environmental Protection Agency (where he helped negotiate the 1992 Framework Convention on Climate Change) and was a senior fellow at the Peterson Institute for International Economics in Washington, DC. From 2011 to 2014, he served as commissioner of Connecticut's Department of Energy and Environmental Protection.

Mariel Ferro Rivas is a management science PhD candidate at Tecnológico de Monterrey's EGADE Business School. She holds a public accounting and finance degree from the Tecnológico de

Monterrey, Campus Tampico, and a master's degree in business management, with a minor in marketing, from the Universidad Virtual del Tecnológico de Monterrey. Her research focuses on entrepreneurship and corporate sustainability.

Aideé Figueroa López holds a PhD in management science from Tecnológico de Monterrey's EGADE Business School. She is an energy engineer and holds two master's degrees in engineering and finance. Her research interests include corporate sustainability and management with a focus on the automotive and energy sectors. She has extensive experience working as a project and planning manager for several companies in the chemical and automotive sectors.

Edwin Garcia is a Gruber Fellow in Global Justice working at the Fundación Cordillera Tropical in Ecuador. He is developing a management plan for a "Green Highway" within the Sangay National Park. He graduated from the Yale School of Forestry and Environmental Studies with a master of environmental management degree. Prior to attending Yale, Garcia worked at the landscape design firm Mingo Design LLC. He holds an MS in industrial engineering from NYU and a BE from the University of Cuenca.

Margarita Heredia Soto has a PhD in social and economic sciences from Johannes Kepler University in Linz, Austria. Dr. Heredia has more than 17 years of experience working in roles where business and academia develop responsible solutions that positively influence corporate results and society. She has specialized in strategy, leadership, marketing, shared value, and international business. Dr. Heredia is the author of the book *The Influence of Malinchismo on Mexican Consumers*.

Siegfried King works in the agricultural sector in Chile. He trained as a mechanical engineer with experience in the renewables and energy efficiency sectors. He graduated from Yale with a master of environmental management degree, focusing on corporate sustainability. He is a recipient of a Fulbright scholarship and the EDF Climate Corps fellowship. He was a participant in the 2017 UNLEASH innovation lab in Denmark, where 1,000 young leaders from around the world worked together on the Sustainable Development Goals and the links between food production, water, and energy.

Fairuz O. Loutfi Olivares is advisor to the German Cooperation for Sustainable Development (GIZ) in Mexico and is a lecturer at the Universidad Iberoamericana in Mexico City. She previously worked for four years as the advisor to the undersecretary of electricity at Mexico's Secretariat of Energy. She graduated with a master of environmental management degree from the Yale School of Forestry and Environmental Studies. In 2016, she contributed to a market potential report on the feasibility of renewable thermal technologies in Connecticut. She has extensive corporate sustainability experience, including as an EDF Climate Corps fellow exploring energy-saving opportunities at Legrand North America's manufacturing facility in Tijuana, Mexico. Fairuz graduated with honors from Universidad Iberoamericana, Mexico City, with a bachelor's degree in mechatronics and production engineering. In 2015, she attended the COP21 climate change conference as member of the UN Economic Commission for Latin America and the Caribbean (ECLAC) delegation.

Felipe Perez is a full professor at INCAE Business School in Nicaragua. A Salvadoran native, he holds a PhD in agricultural economics from Purdue University, where he specialized in natural resource economics and business strategy. He also holds an MBA from INCAE Business School, with a concentration in banking, and an agronomy degree from the Autonomous University of Chapingo, Mexico. His research interests include corporate social responsibility and competitiveness, sustainability and agribusiness, business innovation, and sustainable business at the base of the pyramid. Dr. Perez previously headed INCAE's Agro-Industry Program, directed the Export-Nicaragua program at the Center for Entrepreneurship, and continues to teach for INCAE's programs at campuses in Nicaragua and Costa Rica. Perez is also an international consultant and advisor to several companies in

Latin America, and serves on the board of two Central American firms in the agribusiness sector.

Hellen Quinonez is the Head of the Administrative Liaison Department for the National Institute of Social Economy in Mexico and is a PhD student in business administration at the EGADE Business School in Mexico City. Her thesis explores social enterprises, specifically hybrid organizations. She has a BS in agronomy engineering from the Monterrey Institute of Technology and Higher Education, and two master's degrees, one in plant sciences from the Hebrew University of Jerusalem and a second in administration from EGADE Business School. She has previously worked for several agricultural companies in Mexico.

Francisco Gabriel Rodríguez González is an associate professor at Universidad de las Americas Puebla in Mexico. He holds a PhD in business administration from EGADE Business School, Mexico City, where he specialized in operations management and continuous improvement. He also holds an MBA from EGADE Business School, Mexico City, with a concentration in strategy, and a bachelor's degree in business administration from the Universidad del Valle de Mexico, Tlalpan. Dr. Rodríguez's professional experience includes more than 10 years working as a business consultant in public and private organizations. His research interests focus on process improvement, eco-efficiency, and eco-innovation, as well as corporate sustainability. He has authored and coauthored several scientific publications, including an entry in the SAGE Encyclopedia of Quality and the Service Economy. He is part of the team that won the European Foundation for Management Development (EFMD) Case Writing Competition 2017, in the "Continuous Improvement: The Journey to Excellence" category.

INTRODUCTION

Daniel C. Esty

Business leaders in the twentieth century focused on delivering share-holder value. They paid attention to top-line growth and bottom-line success. Environmental degradation emerged as a concern in the 1990s across the corporate world, including in Latin America. But while pollution impacts, ecosystem vitality, and natural resource management became top-tier *policy* concerns in recent decades, those topics remained secondary priorities for almost all companies until very recently. Executives in major enterprises viewed environmental matters as a regulatory compliance issue to be dealt with by lawyers and engineers.

Business attitudes toward the environment—encompassing energy use and the broad range of topics associated with *sustainability*—have now shifted dramatically. Today's leading executives understand that their companies have social responsibilities. Of course, they are still accountable to their shareholders. But understanding that business success cannot be achieved at the expense of society means companies must also answer to an array of other stakeholders—from customers to employees to the communities in which they operate and, indeed, to society more broadly.

This obligation takes on new importance in the context of emerging *planetary boundaries*. As Johan Rockström and his colleagues at the Stockholm Resilience Center have highlighted, human-induced stress on various Earth systems threatens to push the planet beyond its "safe operating space" along a number of dimensions—from climate change to biodiversity to water availability and ocean acidification.[1] In addition to these ecological threats that may impinge on the quality of life on Earth, other researchers have identified a set of social strains—including poverty, income inequality, and evolving employment structures—that threaten the fabric of our communities.[2] Where at one time this entire agenda would have been seen as the purview of governments, business today shares responsibility for society's response. As Peter Bakker, president of the World Business Council for Sustainable Development (WBCSD) and former CEO of the Dutch logistics company TNT, likes to say, "Businesses cannot succeed in societies that fail."[3]

Simply put, a *sustainability imperative* now looms over the business world.[4] This book offers guidance on how to manage the various dimensions of this sustainability agenda—providing lessons from a dozen case studies across Spanish-speaking Latin America and the sustainability management literature more generally. Of course, the optimal response to sustainability will vary by industry and geography. Countries in Latin America—as in every region—each have their own distinct economic, political, and environmental contexts. In recent decades, economies in the region have grown, incomes have risen, and poverty rates have fallen. But progress remains uneven and inequality remains high, leading to a wide range of environmental priorities across Latin America.

Because of these trends, corporate sustainability in Latin America is sure to develop in its own unique form. With chapters that draw on real-world corporate experiences in addressing environment, energy, and social issues in Chile, Colombia, the Dominican Republic, Ecuador, Honduras, Mexico, and Nicaragua, this volume represents the first comprehensive study of corporate sustainability in the Latin American context. It highlights the challenges, opportunities, and best practices of companies from Chile to Mexico—and blazes a trail for others to follow.

Corporate Social Responsibility Is Not Enough

While the concept of *corporate social responsibility* (CSR) gained some traction in Latin America in the early 2000s, business leaders have now come to realize that a CSR focus is not enough. Making contributions to schools or sports programs or hospitals does not compensate for causing environmental harm. Being less bad is not good enough. Companies today, of course, must avoid being seen as a source of toxic exposures or land degradation. But increasingly, they are also expected to do more.

The need for business to address environmental challenges has been articulated with a variety of vocabularies and theoretical frameworks around the world. Commentators in the United States often speak of *corporate sustainability* and sometimes (although less often in recent years) corporate social responsibility. Western European observers may refer to the concept of *ecological modernization* and its emphasis on private sector innovation increasing sustainability while continuing to foster economic growth. What these approaches share is the understanding that companies can—and must—be part of the solution to sustainability challenges.

This expanded role creates new opportunities, but it also imposes new obligations. Fundamentally, issues that might once have been delegated to middle managers or technical experts have become matters of strategic importance. Thus, corporate leaders now understand that how they address pollution control, waste management, greenhouse gas emissions, land use, and energy consumption may determine their success in the marketplace. As a result, many large firms now have chief sustainability officers. And almost all companies of any scale recognize that environmental issues cannot be relegated to compliance officers but rather must be addressed by C-suite executives with broad business mandates.

Latin American companies are increasingly recognizing these opportunities and obligations. For example, sustainability became a core concern at Walmart Mexico as the company worked to rehabilitate its public image after a 2012 scandal involving potentially improper payments to speed up the issuance of construction permits. At Mabesa, deepening public environmental consciousness drove the creation of a promising new product line. Solar energy was the central product upon which Tecnosol built its business in Nicaragua. Corporate sustainability came more slowly to Latin America than to Europe or North America, but this collection of cases shows that it is now firmly established.

Sustainability, as this volume explains in detail, has become an important source of *competitive advantage*—or, if mismanaged, *disadvantage*. As the chapters that follow demonstrate, many companies today are bringing a sustainability lens to the full range of their business strategies. In doing so, they are finding ways to reduce risks, cut costs, drive growth, and build their brands. More and more companies are finding that their sustainability initiatives deliver both measurable contributions to profitability and intangible value through enhanced customer loyalty, employee engagement, and trust in the marketplace. This volume walks through these various sustainability "plays" in the following pages— and provides case studies of how to deliver on these opportunities in the chapters that make up this volume. It also highlights the challenges and potential pitfalls of bringing a focus on energy and environmental issues into corporate strategy—thus providing a guide to what I call the *labyrinth* of sustainability.

Changing Public Expectations

Companies might once have been seen as good corporate citizens if they complied with applicable laws and regulations. But meeting legal obligations is now just a starting point. As governments around the world have struggled to keep up with environmental challenges and rising public expectations, society has begun to look to the corporate world for help in delivering safe drinking water, improved sanitation, reduced air pollution, better waste management, clean energy, and other environmental amenities.

Business leaders are stepping into this expanded role. A recent survey of Fortune 500 CEOs, including a number of Latin American business leaders, found that only 4 percent agreed with the Milton Friedman-esque statement: "my company should mainly focus on making profits, and not be distracted by social goals." Forty-three percent rejected this narrow perspective and said their company "should actively seek ways to address major social problems as a core part of our business strategy."[5]

These new expectations about the role of business, which have emerged over the past several decades, are increasingly being formalized.

For example, the 2015 Paris Climate Change Agreement shifts the focus of efforts to reduce greenhouse gas emissions from a top-down approach that relied on national governments to lead the way toward a clean energy future to a bottom-up strategy that recognizes the need for "broader engagement," including by cities, states and provinces, and *companies*.[6] Thus, business leaders, alongside mayors and governors, are now on the front lines in the battle to reduce greenhouse gas emissions and to mitigate the threat of global warming and associated sea level rise, increased intensity and frequency of hurricanes and other wind storms, changed rainfall patterns, more frequent droughts and floods, and diminished agricultural productivity.

What drove this shift? First, it became clear that the top-down approach wasn't working. Emissions were continuing to rise across the world, including in Latin America. Second, it turns out that presidents and prime ministers don't have much day-to-day control over the carbon footprints of their societies. Thus, as countries develop the details of their *nationally determined contributions* (NDCs) to climate change action in fulfillment of the 2015 Paris commitments, they are increasingly focusing on strategies being delivered by cities, states, and companies.

Indeed, with regard to the important role business must play, the Paris Agreement seeks to "[enhance] public and private sector participation in the implementation of nationally determined contributions."[7] Thus, many business leaders are developing their own climate change action plans—and looking for ways that their companies might obtain marketplace rewards by delivering clean energy solutions in particular and solving the environmental problems of their customers more generally. As the case study in this volume on Nissan's Mexican auto factories explains, Nissan has made a reduced corporate carbon footprint a global priority for the company—as it seeks to appeal to the driving public as a provider of cutting-edge vehicles.

Likewise, the Sustainable Development Goals (SDGs) adopted by the United Nations in 2015 as a policy framework for the world community spell out 17 areas of specific focus from poverty alleviation to clean water and sanitation as well as affordable and clean energy—many of which will require private sector implementation. Each of these "global goals" has a defined set of quantitative targets, providing

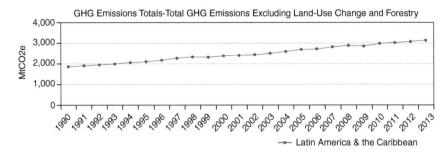

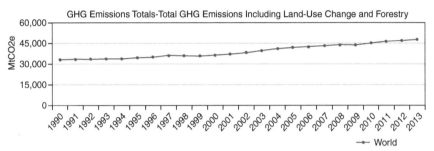

Greenhouse gas (GHG) emissions in millions of metric tons of carbon dioxide equivalent (MtCO2e).

Source: World Resources Institute CAIT Historic Data.

a mechanism to gauge progress to help guide companies toward a sustainable future.

As with the 2015 Paris Climate Change Agreement, the important role that business must play in delivering results under the SDGs has been explicitly recognized. In adopting the SDGs, the UN General Assembly concluded "that the active participation of the private sector can contribute to the achievement of sustainable development, including through the important tool of public-private partnerships," emphasizing corporate sustainability reporting.[8] Tools are now being developed to help companies align their business strategies with the SDGs and then to track their contributions to progress on each of the global goals. For instance, the SDG Compass, developed by the Global Reporting Initiative (GRI), the WBCSD, and the UN Global Compact, provides a detailed game plan for helping companies (1) understand the SDGs, (2) define their priorities, (3) set goals, (4) integrate the SDGs into their core business strategy, and (5) report on their internal progress.[9]

The companies featured in this book show the importance of being forward-thinking—and seeing environmental problems as sustainability *opportunities*. Grupo Vanguardia's innovative recycling program, for example, demonstrates the possibility of generating new revenue streams while providing solutions to a pressing environmental challenge. And companies like Walmart and Las Palmas have used their sustainability strategies not only to mitigate their exposure to climate change but also to reduce their reputational risks and to better engage with the communities in which they operate. Community engagement strategies such as these are essential for business leaders in any region—and especially in Latin America where historical distrust of multinational corporations remains potent in some countries and communities.

Sustainability-Minded Investors

Changing public expectations about the role of business are playing out in financial markets as well. Specifically, the rise of mainstream investors who care about the Environmental/Social/Governance (ESG) performance of the companies in their portfolios provides another force that has sharpened the focus on sustainability for companies listed on stock markets. Interest in sustainability screening and impact investing has ramped up dramatically over the past few years. The fact that more than 1,200 investment and asset managers, representing over US$59 trillion in assets under management, have committed to the United Nations Principles for Responsible Investment (PRI) initiative offers one measure of this trend. In the United States, the Governance and Accountability Institute estimates that 447 institutional investors, 300 money managers, and 1,043 community investment institutions are now available to those who want to put their values into their financial choices.[10]

A growing number of these ESG investors are asking to see performance indicators that highlight which companies are making progress on sustainability issues—and which are not. More and more investment advisors and fund managers have therefore decided to drop from their portfolios companies that have significant "carbon exposure" or other unaddressed environmental shortcomings.[11] Some fund managers, such as David Blood at Generation Investment Management, have developed "green alpha" investment strategies—buying shares in companies seen as sustainability leaders on the theory that this leadership position will translate into stock market outperformance.[12] And while sustainable finance has been slow to take hold in Latin America, as more reliable indicators become available, it is widely expected to pick up across the continent.[13]

Not all investors and financial advisors scrutinize ESG performance with the same goals in mind.[14] Some simply want to avoid climate change exposure. Others care about a broader range of environmental issues, or about social issues, such as diversity in the workforce or a company's track record in working with labor unions. How far these investors push their sustainability values also varies. Some insist on excluding "bad actor" companies from their portfolios even if the result is more volatility in their investment results and lower returns over time. Others push their ESG interests only to the point where their investment returns are not significantly affected. In any case, the sharp rise in investor ESG interest gives companies another big reason to bring a focus on sustainability into their day-to-day business strategy.

Sustainability Leaders

What are companies doing to get ahead of the sustainability curve? A lot—as the case studies that follow make clear. Taken as a whole, the companies profiled in this book demonstrate that successful sustainability strategies must be tailored to the specific industry and market circumstances. These strategies also span a spectrum of levels of commitment and difficulty. They range from relatively easy "win-win" opportunities, such as increased energy efficiency, to more transformational and challenging efforts to integrate sustainability into core corporate strategy. The cases in the chapters that follow depict companies working across the breadth of this spectrum. Walmart Mexico, for instance, reduced its energy costs though wind power—a clear win-win. On the other hand, in the wake of Hurricane Georges and with the prospect of more frequent and intense windstorms looming, Rizek

Cacao saw an opportunity to overhaul its business model and focus on sustainable cocoa production. No single formula will work in all situations. Our research, however, has identified four main categories of sustainability-driven competitive advantage: (1) risk reduction, (2) cost savings, (3) growth, and (4) intangible value.

Risk Management

BP's 2010 Deepwater Horizon disaster, which killed 11 people and spilled over 200 million gallons of oil into the Gulf of Mexico, vividly demonstrates how much damage poorly managed environmental risks can inflict. Not only did the blowout devastate marine life across a wide swath of the northern Gulf, it cost the company tens of billions of dollars in cleanup costs, legal fees, fines, natural resource damage compensation, and payments to those injured by the spill. BP was also subject to—and continues to face—consumer boycotts, nongovernmental organization (NGO) denunciations, media criticism, and other threats to its social license to operate.

Latin America has seen its share of similar environmental disasters and risk management failures. In Brazil, the 2015 Samarco dam collapse—which caused a massive mudslide that resulted in 19 deaths, destruction of a number of villages, and flooding of a vast area with mining waste—has already cost the co-owners of the operation, BHP Billiton and Vale, more than US$10 billion in legal fees and cleanup costs. And the companies face ongoing criminal legal proceedings and government reviews.

Inadequate risk management can emerge in other forms that are equally costly. Failing to meet regulatory standards, for example, often leads to substantial fines and penalties. In this regard, VW's legal bill for its tailpipe emissions cheating scandal now exceeds US$22 billion, including settlements and fines.[15] Beyond the financial price the company has paid, VW has a number of executives facing criminal prosecution. Moreover, the company's market value dropped by US$20 billion in the wake of the scandal.[16]

Changed regulatory requirements represent another dimension of risk, which can translate into new costs and competitive disadvantage. The fact that many countries are putting a price (in one of any number of forms) on greenhouse gas emissions in the wake of the 2015 Paris Climate Change Agreement has spurred interest among investors and market analysts in the *carbon intensity* of companies, especially in comparison to their industry peers. This focus anticipates the prospect that some corporations will be relatively advantaged and others disadvantaged by tightening climate change controls. Those companies that have been paying attention to energy efficiency and taking up opportunities to switch away from fossil fuels to renewable sources of electricity are likely to be the winners from this regulatory evolution. Several of the companies profiled in this book—including Tecnosol in Nicaragua as well as Grupo Herdez, Walmart, and Nissan Mexico— demonstrate this phenomenon.

Eco-efficiency and Resource Productivity as a Pathway to Cost Savings

Perhaps no area of activity in the world of sustainable business has gotten more attention than the opportunity for cost savings from energy efficiency. Companies of all sizes have seen their operating costs reduced through investments in LED bulbs and other high-efficiency lighting, modernized equipment, and other energy efficiency initiatives. But these eco-efficiency opportunities to do more with less go beyond electricity. Manufacturers that reduce scrap or reuse waste materials often find cost savings that go straight to the bottom line—as the chapters on Vanguardia's recycling experience in Honduras and CENTROSUR's reduction and reuse of scrap in Ecuador demonstrate.

More efficient use of water can be another source of cost savings, particularly in water-intensive industries, such as agriculture. The case study on Las Palmas, a Chilean avocado orchard, demonstrates the potential gains in this regard. Nestlé's work with its supply chain in Mexico on water conservation and sustainable agriculture adds depth to this line of logic as does the case study of Bavaria's water management strategy related to its beer production in Colombia.

Smart companies look for efficiency savings up and down their value chains. Some companies, such as Walmart, have found significant cost-cutting opportunities *upstream* by bringing eco-efficiency strategies to their suppliers. Rizek's work with its 4,000 independent cocoa farmers across the Dominican Republic offers another example of this principle in action. Others have uncovered cost savings *downstream* through better shipping and logistics—or improved customer sustainability. The Ecuadorian energy company CENTROSUR, for example, developed a revolutionary sustainability program designed to encourage its customers to replace outdated and energy inefficient refrigerators, all while generating invaluable data about the company's complex supply chain.

Sustainability-Driven Growth in Revenues and Profit Margins

Companies that use their sustainability strategies to drive innovation and meet their customers' sustainability needs are often able to achieve dramatic revenue growth. Latin America has witnessed a number of success stories of this sort. Indeed, the chapter on Mabesa's Bio Baby disposable diaper, which has allowed the company to expand sales across Mexico and now in other markets, including the United States, shows how sustainability leadership can translate into major market opportunities.

Sustainability strategies can also be a way to differentiate a product or service and add *value* from the customer's perspective, thereby allowing more pricing flexibility and higher profit margins. In this regard, Mabesa was able to take advantage of an unfilled gap in the market for high quality and sustainable diapers, developing and marketing a new product that is now sold across Latin America and the United States in partnership with Walmart.

Sustainability-driven growth strategies must, of course, be managed carefully. As the case studies in this volume make clear, companies will not succeed with a *green marketing* or *sustainability* sales focus unless their products meet consumer quality and price expectations. But eco-marketing can make sense as a "third button" to push with consumers, especially where the market has a growing LOHAS (lifestyle of health and sustainability) dimension.[17] While Latin America's LOHAS market segment remains smaller than in Europe or North America, it is now expanding, as the Grupo Herdez case study makes clear.

Brand Trust and Intangible Value

Some corporate sustainability strategies pay off *indirectly* through their impact on a company's reputation and brand value. In a world where the public expects companies to be responsible corporate citizens and leaders on environmental and social concerns, business executives have come to recognize that they ignore sustainability at their peril. Indeed, companies that fail to meet the rising environmental and social expectations of markets can find themselves at risk of losing their social license to operate. Those who exceed expectations can anticipate not just public approval but government support, as the Nissan case study highlights.

Sustainability leadership can translate into brand perceptions and intangible value in a number of ways—both positive and negative. Trust has always been a critical factor in consumer decisions about who to buy products from. In today's hyper-connected world with social media commentators ready to pounce on corporate misdeeds, thoughtful environmental management and good sustainability practices are critical to avoid problems that can damage a brand and destroy public trust. As Warren Buffett has famously observed, "It takes 20 years to build a reputation, and only five minutes to ruin it." Lapses in sustainability management thus require quick action as the Walmart case below highlights. In particular, after an investigation by the *New York Times* revealed a history of improper dealings with Mexican officials, Walmart had to overhaul its sustainability strategy as a way to publicly demonstrate a commitment to avoid any hint of corruption going forward.

Similarly, recent research suggests that companies seen as "doing the right thing" on environmental and social issues develop a more loyal customer base.[18] Nissan had such a theory in mind when it insisted that all of its production platforms, including its factories in Mexico, adopt the Nissan Green Program focused on reducing environmental impacts, shrinking the company's carbon footprint, and buying more renewable power. A similar spirit animates Nestlé's commitment to Creating Shared Value (CSV), a strategy of sustainability engagement with the communities in which it operates that the company developed with Harvard Business School Professor Michael Porter.

Companies across Latin America and around the world have begun, moreover, to use sustainability initiatives to attract and retain top-quality employees. Bimbo CEO Daniel Servitje Montull cites the competition for talent as one of the reasons for his company's active commitment to sustainability.[19] Knowledge workers, who want *meaning* and a *sense of purpose* in their work, are particularly likely to care about the sustainability practices of the companies they work for. And indeed, studies show that employees are increasingly concerned about their employers' social and environmental impacts.[20] Thus, as competition for these high-end employees heats up across Latin America and around the world, more and more corporate sustainability strategies are emphasizing employee engagement as an essential value driver.

It's Not Easy Being Green

Corporate sustainability must be understood as a journey rather than a destination. Not every effort to drive strategy from environmental or social issues will pay off. Taking risks will often be required. Learning from experience about what works—and what does not—will be critical. The companies featured in the chapters that follow have all, on balance, been successful in their sustainability efforts—demonstrating that sustainability is indeed creating competitive advantage for Latin American companies. Many of these companies, however, have had to overcome setbacks along the way, and many face continued threats on the horizon. The Grupo Vanguardia chapter, for example, describes difficulties the company faces due to missed growth targets and the loss of business partners. In the Nissan Mexicana case, changes in electricity markets introduced new hurdles for renewable energy expansion. Because of these challenges, our research suggests that companies that achieve the greatest eco-advantages or sustainability-driven competitive strength in the marketplace almost always have a commitment to continuous improvement in their environmental and social programs. They learn from their mistakes—and continually refine their sustainability strategies.

They are also *systematic* and business-like in their pursuit of sustainability advantage. Successful strategies build on a carefully structured review of the range of issues that need to be addressed and rigorous analysis of which issues are most *material* for the company and its industry. My prior books, *Green to Gold* and *The Green to Gold Business Playbook*, provide a set of tools and step-by-step advice on how to carry out an AUDIO analysis (Aspects, Upstream, Downstream, Issues, Opportunities) that ensures robust *issue spotting*—covering present concerns and future risks, matters that arise upstream (with suppliers) and downstream (in distribution or with customers) as well as within a company's own facilities, and turning challenges into opportunities. These books also offer a framework for *stakeholder mapping* to ensure that the sustainability interests of customers, suppliers, employees, investors, industry peers, regulators, communities, political leaders, NGOs, and the media are all factored in to any sustainability plan. Finally, they provide guidance on how to identify the *core capabilities* needed to execute a sustainability plan and how to *fill gaps* that might otherwise undermine implementation.[21]

Keys to Corporate Sustainability Success

The case studies in this volume and the broader corporate sustainability literature suggest that successful corporate sustainability strategies depend on five key factors: (1) leadership, (2) vision and execution, (3) partnering, (4) communications, and (5) inspiration.

Leadership

Leadership from the top emerges as a common feature of all of the case studies in this volume—and from corporate sustainability research more broadly. In a fast-paced business world, where corporate executives face pressure to deliver results across many parameters including top-line growth, cost controls, and improved margins, sustainability initiatives require a *champion* to get traction. In the absence of that leadership, managers will continue to deliver on existing key performance indicators—ignoring the sustainability agenda as a second-tier concern.

In many cases, the champion has been the CEO. In some cases, a chief sustainability officer or other top executive will be positioned to drive the agenda. But only a senior official who commands broad respect across the organization can be expected to deliver success on sustainability efforts. While it helps to have a "Green Team" or a Sustainability Working Group charged with implementing initiatives, our research suggests that high-level leadership is essential.

Vision and Execution

Success also depends on clarity of vision and a well-executed implementation plan. Some companies don't fully understand the emerging dimensions of the *sustainability imperative*—or they fail to think through the implications for their industry and their business strategy. Others do the basic analysis and develop a clear vision, but then fail to deliver on the promise established. Those who do best think through the implications of the sustainability agenda for their business strategy, work hard to translate this vision into an action plan, and then work equally hard to implement it and deliver concrete results.

Our research suggests that execution depends on a strong sense of direction from the top, a well-designed implementation strategy, and incentives for mid-level managers to deliver against clearly defined goals. In this regard, it becomes critical for senior managers to cascade the strategy from the top of the organization to the bottom—ensuring that everyone from the headquarters to the factory floor or distant fields understands the sustainability mission and their own responsibilities for delivering results. In addition, quantitative performance metrics prove over and over again to be helpful. Having sustainability results folded into a manager's key performance indicators (KPIs), annual review, and performance bonus leads systematically to better results.

Unilever, the multinational consumer products company—and one of Latin America's largest enterprises—has focused its business strategy on delivering on a "Sustainable Living Plan" based on former CEO Paul Polman's compelling vision of the importance of sustainability to the future of consumers across the planet. With leadership from the top, Unilever has worked to ensure that all of the company's 170,000 employees in more than 100 countries worldwide understand how sustainability relates to their roles. Everyone on the management team has KPIs based on quantitative targets derived from the overarching plan.

In Latin America, Unilever has emphasized sustainability not only in its operations but also in its brand-building efforts. In this regard, Unilever recently acquired the personal care brands and home care product lines of Quala, a leading sustainability-oriented Latin American consumer goods company, which uses aloe vera as well as keratin, biotin, and argan oil to drive eco-minded consumers to its hair styling and other grooming products. In announcing the Quala deal, Paul Polman observed that the acquisition "reinforces Unilever's commitment to our long-term model of compounding growth and sustainable value creation."[22]

Partnering

Sustainability has multiple dimensions and requires expertise on a wide array of topics. Success in delivering on a sustainability strategy therefore depends on assembling cross-functional teams from within the organization and bringing in strong partners from outside. At the outset, a critical strategic question must be answered for each sustainability initiative: does the effort seek to run ahead of the competition and achieve a sustainability advantage for the company? Or does the initiative achieve its results by working with the competition—to lift the industry's sustainability performance while maintaining a level playing field vis-à-vis competitors?

Walmart's efforts to partner with its suppliers on sustainability-driven cost savings aims to improve the company's competitive position in the marketplace—and further advance its distinctive "everyday low prices" advantage. Likewise, Tecnosol offers its Nicaraguan customers microcredit, guidance on how to optimize operation of its solar arrays, and capacity building as a way to differentiate its solar power products from competing solar companies in the marketplace. On the other hand, Coca-Cola's (and FEMSA's) work with Pepsi and other beverage companies leans in the opposite direction. By seeking to ensure that all marketplace participants achieve sustainability gains together, the companies thereby insulate the industry as a whole from criticism of its packaging waste, contributions to obesity, and other environmental and social shortcomings.

For some companies, working with industry peers has proven to be helpful, as FEMSA's sustainability initiatives demonstrate. In other cases, partnering with a knowledgeable NGO has helped a company to understand its sustainability challenges, build public trust, and lift its game accordingly. Bavaria's work with the World Wildlife Fund shows how partnership with an environmental group can pay off. Some companies have also found it advantageous to partner with government entities. Nissan's collaboration with the city and state governments in Aguascalientes to build biogas and wind power generating capacity to power its auto factories and fulfill the company-wide commitment to renewable energy offers a vivid example of how such partnerships can deliver value.

Communications

Our research suggests that a number of companies have developed strong sustainability programs but have had trouble "telling their story" and thus have not gotten full credit for their environmental, energy, or social leadership. We therefore conclude that every sustainability strategy or initiative needs a strong communications dimension. One part of the communications plan needs to focus on internal audiences to make sure that the company's employees and everyone else associated with the enterprise are aware of what is being done—and positioned to help share the story. Even more important is the external communication strategy which needs to be designed to reach all of the company's critical audiences including customers, suppliers, government officials, NGOs, academic partners and other thought leaders, as well as the media. The detail and depth of the narrative provided can vary depending on the audience, but a consistent substantive story emerges as essential. In today's social media world, any inconsistencies will be quickly highlighted—fundamentally damaging efforts to get the message out.

Inspiration

Sustainability strategies that *inspire* deliver the most successful outcomes. As noted earlier, a growing number of employees want to be part of an enterprise that seeks to make the world a better place. Thus, while developing the "business case" for elements of any sustainability plan is important, ensuring that the vision is uplifting should also be emphasized. With the *sustainability imperative* providing wind beneath the wings and a commitment to a business-like strategy, companies can do good *and* do well. We hope that this book provides some inspiration and guidance for those who take up this mission.

Chapter 1

WATER CONSERVATION IN SCARCITY CONDITIONS: CORPORATE SUSTAINABILITY AT MEXICO'S FEMSA GROUP

Roger Nion Conaway and
Francisco Gabriel Rodríguez González

Abstract

FEMSA Group, a beverage and retail company headquartered in Monterrey, Mexico, has incorporated sustainability into its core business strategy with a special focus on water resource management. This case explores how a multinational corporation relying heavily on water resources can operate in a water-scarce region, advancing conservation and securing a "social license to operate." It also examines the range of water conservation measures the company has instituted and maps out how FEMSA has created economic, social, and environmental value for the communities where the business operates. This success has emerged, in part, through partnerships with like-minded nongovernmental organizations and other for-profit companies. The FEMSA experience thus demonstrates that corporations working in concert with other stakeholders will often improve sustainability performance and business results.

Introduction

FEMSA Group (*Fomento Económico Mexicano, S.A.B. de C.V*) began operations in 1890 and has since emerged as a major beverage and retail company with its base in Monterrey, Mexico. FEMSA now operates in 12 countries, registers annual revenues of over US$18 billion, and employs more than 260,000 people.[1] Its conservation and sustainability efforts serve as a beacon of corporate social responsibility in Mexico.

FEMSA's emphasis on sustainability has emerged partly out of necessity. As the operator of the world's largest independent Coca-Cola bottling enterprise, as well as a stakeholder in Heineken, FEMSA Group must steward the most vital ingredient in its beverages—water. To that end, the company created the nonprofit FEMSA Foundation in 2008 to balance environmental protection, social responsibility, and economic growth. The FEMSA Foundation not only works to conserve water resources, but also delivers a broad array of social benefits to the local communities around FEMSA facilities, including nutrition training, clean water, and sanitation infrastructure. Our discussions with FEMSA and FEMSA Foundation employees have shown that the corporate value of sustainable water commitments extends beyond just securing a company's supply of a key resource.

This case study highlights the water conservation activities of the FEMSA Foundation and the closely related Monterrey Water Fund, known in Spanish as *Fondo de Agua Metropolitano de Monterrey*. Our findings come from three sources: (1) interviews with FEMSA Foundation directors in Monterrey, who oversee activities in the Río San Juan watershed and build partnerships with nongovernmental organizations (NGOs) and funding organizations; (2) notes from firsthand observations during a visit to the watershed in the mountains above Monterrey; and (3) secondary sources accessed through online databases and websites, including FEMSA vision and mission statements.

This chapter explains the evolution of sustainability thinking at FEMSA, then describes the water fund and analyzes its water conservation work in the Monterrey watershed. It details the reforestation efforts, soil restoration activities, and social programs that support families living within the watershed. The chapter also highlights FEMSA's collaboration with other companies, NGOs, and community groups to protect water resources.

FEMSA's Best Practices

FEMSA's commitment to a broad range of social and environmental programs beyond its core business operations is a best practice in corporate sustainability. The company illustrates the benefits of collaborating with public and private partners to deliver such programs. Inaction by the Mexican government led FEMSA to begin addressing critical community water management needs, both as a corporation and through its corporate foundation. For FEMSA and a number of other businesses, acting in the place of underperforming government entities has become a fundamental necessity—and a critical dimension of corporate social responsibility, especially in a developing country setting.

A number of scholars have highlighted the necessity of creating a "stakeholder framework for analyzing and evaluating corporate social performance."[2] Indeed, inclusively creating value for all stakeholders helps develop intangible assets. These assets provide competitive advantage and increase shareholder wealth.[3] FEMSA's sustainability strategy reflects such a "stakeholder" framework by integrating economic goals with social and environmental activities. This approach secures the company's social license to operate. In a 2007 article, John Campbell of Dartmouth College and Copenhagen Business School asked, "Why would corporations behave in socially responsible ways?"[4] The answer, he wrote, is that the financial health of an individual corporation depends on the success of the economy as a whole. FEMSA's sustainability strategy and the efforts of the FEMSA Foundation provide a vivid example of Campbell's argument in action.

Sustainability at FEMSA

The FEMSA Group published its first sustainability report in 2005. These reports are published separately from the company's annual report and are publicly available online. This outreach has proven to be an effective communications strategy, signaling a commitment to transparency and building community trust.

The group's sustainability reports conform to Global Reporting Initiative G4 guidelines, an internationally accepted framework for measuring triple bottom line performance. The guidelines helped the company to identify a series of potential issues that could also pose business risks for its Coca-Cola FEMSA unit:

- changes in consumer preferences;
- water scarcity and inability to keep existing water concessions;
- risk of raw material price hikes;
- significant changes in regulatory or fiscal regimens; and
- competition that could affect Coca-Cola FEMSA's performance.

This reporting helped focus FEMSA's sustainability strategy on water and other related issues. In 2012, FEMSA made additional changes in order to create the company's "Strategic Sustainability Framework." The values that emerged from a materiality analysis helped sharpen the FEMSA Group's focus on three sustainability pillars: "People, Planet, Community."[5] These priorities align FEMSA's ethics and values strategy with the *sustainability imperative* identified by Lubin and Esty.[6] FEMSA's water conservation activities have emerged from these values.

The FEMSA Foundation and Water Funds

The FEMSA Foundation's water initiative began in 2008, seeking to achieve "the conservation and sustainable use of water and the improvement of quality of life in the community through education, science, and applied technology."[7] Because it recognizes the importance of community needs, and not just the company's own priorities, the foundation has also long championed nutrition in conjunction with water issues. To deliver on its water conservation and access goals, the foundation launched a series of water funds supported by the Latin American Water Funds Partnership.

A water fund oversees water-related environmental services and promotes water protection as a locally organized nongovernmental institution. Water funds serve as an example of "alternative action," born in civil society when government inaction leaves communities' needs unmet. Water funds can offer management efficiency and sustainability for threatened watersheds. For FEMSA, water funds serve as trust funds that collect private contributions for watershed interventions and community services.

The FEMSA Foundation's water funds integrate well within FEMSA Group's triple bottom line sustainability perspective. The funds help the company deliver: (1) social development, such as economic improvements to watershed residents' lives; (2) environmental sustainability, focusing on reforestation and protecting water sources from soil erosion; and (3) increased economic value for FEMSA. This commitment to community success as well as profitability has underpinned FEMSA's business model for nearly a decade, and ensured the company's social license to operate.

FEMSA has also worked with the Latin American Water Funds Partnership to expand its reach. The partnership is comprised of four organizations: the FEMSA Foundation, the Global Environment Facility, The Nature Conservancy, and the Inter-American Development Bank. It has set out to create 32 local water funds in Latin America and preserve 3 million hectares of land (approximately 7.5 million acres). Fifteen million people will benefit from new environmental services the water funds make possible. In 2014, the Rockefeller Foundation recognized the partnership with its Next Century Innovators Award.

In Monterrey, Hurricane Alex accelerated the growth of these partnerships, as in June 2010 the hurricane caused massive flooding and extensive infrastructure damage. The deluge led the partnership to develop extensive water conservation activities in the mountains surrounding Monterrey. The federal government failed to respond quickly or adequately, hindering local government efforts, so the private sector took responsibility. As we explain below, the Monterrey Water Fund was key to FEMSA's efforts.

Sustainability Analysis: The Monterrey Water Fund

The impact of FEMSA's sustainability efforts is perhaps best illustrated by the Monterrey Water Fund, an effort to protect water quality and improve livelihoods in FEMSA's home region. The fund focuses on the

building of water infrastructure, reforestation, and the creation of economic incentives for conservation for local landowners.

Water Flow around Monterrey

The Río San Juan watershed encompasses the states of Coahuila and
Tamaulipas in addition to FEMSA's home state of Nuevo León and
Monterrey, its capital. The watershed serves approximately five million
people. Water availability in the region, however, is low and irregular,
and water sources have faced issues due to pollution. In a 2011 article,
José Cháidez demonstrated how sustainable management of the Río
San Juan's water remains critical to addressing the demand for agricultural, industrial, and municipal freshwater consumption, as well as
natural disaster management.[8]

In interviews with the authors of this chapter, local residents described
Monterrey's strange relationship with water. Because the city and land
nearby do not receive much rain, highway and bridge designs do not
consider the impact of excess water during storms. Such inadequate
infrastructure has led to a growing inability to manage extreme water
events. In recent decades, Monterrey has faced two significant flooding
incidents: Hurricane Gilbert in 1988, and Hurricane Alex in 2010.
Hurricane Alex struck Monterrey with a peak water discharge around
15 percent lower than the peak during Hurricane Gilbert, yet the resulting
water flows resulted in more significant damage to infrastructure. This
counterintuitive impact resulted from the degradation of the surrounding
environment. First, the upper watershed forest and soil health had declined
between 1988 and 2010. Forest fires and tree diseases had damaged the
watershed forest, and water ran down hillsides rather than soaking into the
soil. Second, Monterrey's rapid population growth resulted in unorgan-
ized and unplanned development. Concrete streets, asphalt parking lots,
and other urban development prevented water absorption in formerly
forested mountain areas. Finally, accumulated water funneled through the
city through only one source, the Santa Catarina River.

The combination of these three factors has increased the intensity
of water flow during extreme weather events. To address the increased

risk of flooding, the local government constructed a 70-meter-high peak-breaker dam in 2007 at a cost of 530 million pesos (US$45 million). The dam regulates water flow into the Santa Catarina River, intending to slow water flow during heavy rainfall and hurricanes. Even so, Monterrey suffered significant flooding during Hurricane Alex— engineers have said that without the dam, flooding would have resulted in more significant damage.

The Formation of the Monterrey Water Fund

The Monterrey Water Fund was launched in 2013 as an NGO dedicated to addressing the water challenges highlighted by Hurricane Alex. The fund began with the participation of the Latin American Water Funds Partnership, the FEMSA Foundation, and The Nature Conservancy. In 2016, the government asked the Monterrey Water Fund to develop the Water Plan for the state of Nuevo León, where Monterrey is located. This request allowed the Monterrey Water Fund to influence watershed protection around the sprawling metropolis of Monterrey.

   At the beginning of the planning process, two groups were created: one technical and another political. The major stakeholders included the Tecnológico de Monterrey (a private university), the Universidad Autónoma de Nuevo León (a public university), CONAGUA (the national water authority), SEMARNAT (the national environmental authority), CONAFOR (the national forestry authority), state agencies like the water utility of Nuevo León, and local governments like the Monterrey Municipality. NGOs took part as well, including *Pronatura Noreste* and the *Fondo Mexicano para la Conservación de la Naturaleza*, the largest fund for conservation issues in Mexico. In the two years prior to the public launch, the water fund held meetings and workshops, shared information, and conducted analyses.

   The Monterrey Water Fund received funding from the Natural Capital Project, a group formed by The Nature Conservancy, the World Wildlife Fund, Stanford University, and the University of Minnesota. This group developed a software platform to identify areas in the Río San Juan watershed where environmental intervention measures would have maximum impact. Two consulting firms, KPMG and Baker & McKenzie, developed the governance of the fund. Membership and participation emerged as a particular strength: major companies in Monterrey, such as FEMSA, CEMEX, Arca Continental, Heineken, Cuprum, and Alfa, joined the initiative.

The Monterrey Water Fund is organized as a trust fund. Three committees form its foundation. The science and technology committee, led by Alfa, which reviews the Conservation Plan developed by national government agencies and then presents it to the board; the communication committee, led by Arca Continental and Heineken; and the fundraising committee, led by FEMSA Foundation. The board itself consists of a president or CEO from each company. The president of Cuprum, an aluminum manufacturer, serves as chairman.[9] Long-time FEMSA competitors such as PepsiCo also collaborate as members of the water fund.

The water fund aims to safeguard the water security of the state of Nuevo León. It has four specific objectives: (1) to reduce flooding risk and maintain a discharge rate of under 15 cubic meters of water per second to the local Santa Catarina River during a hurricane; (2) to improve water infiltration in the upper watershed; (3) to provide education to nurture a culture of water awareness in Monterrey; and (4) to draw more public funding to continue the conservation of the watershed. The fund aims to maximize its return on investment by dedicating resources to the conservation measures that are most needed in the Río San Juan watershed.

The Activities of the Monterrey Water Fund

To accomplish its goal of improved watershed health, the Monterrey Water Fund invests in solutions for improved water flow, incentivizes local landowners and residents to support conservation, and ensures long-term improvement of water quality via reforestation efforts.

The water fund has supported projects throughout the Monterrey basin. These efforts include soil restoration, reforestation, fence building, and the development of trenches, ditches, and closed ponds (*tinas ciegas*), which slow the flow of water down mountainsides. These solutions enable more efficient water infiltration into the soil and prevent sediment from washing into water sources and disrupting ecosystems. Workers have also placed gabion mesh—made of high tensile wire coated with a thick corrosion-resistant layer of zinc—to slow soil loss in places where bare dirt is eroding. The fund has also financed small dams (45 centimeters, or 18 inches, in height) made from dead trees and fallen limbs to support the mountain soil. These dams run horizontally every 15–30 meters across the Monterrey watershed's steepest slopes. The removal of dead wood from the forest also reduces fire risk.

In addition to these environmental activities, the water fund provides economic benefit by employing local residents. Similar efforts also target the large landowners inside the borders of Parque Nacional Cumbres de Monterrey. This national park covers 177,000 hectares (438,000 acres) and contains Monterrey's signature natural formation, *Cerro de la Silla* (Saddle Mountain). By paying the landowners to assist in conservation efforts, the water fund hopes to reduce the prevalence of illegal logging and create incentives for conservation. Landowners receive annual payments tied to their conservation of land.

In order to promote native species restoration, the fund has also mandated that local reforestation projects only use *Pinus pseudostrobus* (white pine) seedlings produced in the national park. Participating organizations must source trees from a local nursery in the upper watershed area, run by local women, called *Mujeres Unidas para la Conservación*. Donations from the water fund to local NGOs like *Pronatura Noreste*, *Reforestación Extrema* and *Reforestamos México* finance these purchases. *Pronatura Noreste* has reported a survival rate of nearly 100 percent for newly planted white pines. All of these efforts can help to increase water availability, improve quality, and reduce the damage caused by storms.

Conclusion

This case study explains the logic behind a company engaging in water conservation activities and advancing a broader environmental and social agenda as part of its core business strategy. FEMSA has identified a complex series of water-related issues that pose threats to its beverage business: water shortages in drought-stricken areas as well as floods that occur when hurricanes surge in from the Gulf of Mexico, inundating cities and coastal areas. Consequently, water conservation and management—and thus a sustainability strategy—became a priority for the company. By examining a specific watershed conservation activity of the FEMSA Foundation and the Monterrey Water Fund, this study illustrates how collaboration and networking among private organizations can strengthen corporate responsibility efforts. These arrangements can serve as examples for other areas of Mexico struggling with similar water issues.

Chapter 2

WALMART MEXICO: CLEAN ENERGY TO REDUCE COSTS AND IMPROVE CORPORATE IMAGE

Mariel Ferro Rivas and Mariana Cesín Sastré

Abstract

Sustainability strategy has become a top business priority for Walmart Mexico, the retail giant's largest company outside of the United States. Walmart Mexico has not always prioritized sustainability. In fact, the company had long relied on a business model that instead emphasized low-cost production, low wages, and limited benefits for its store employees. Walmart Mexico has, however, now embraced sustainability as the centerpiece of a new, community engagement driven approach to business. This sustainability initiative—started as an investment in low-cost renewable energy resources—aligns well with Walmart's underlying commitment to "everyday low prices." These investments also work to improve Walmart's public image, blunting political concerns that had arisen in Mexico about reports of corruption at the company. The case of Walmart Mexico brings to light two important lessons for Latin American companies on sustainability strategy. First, context matters: Walmart's commitment to financial savings actually strengthened the case for cost-saving investments in sustainable energy. Second, a crisis can sometimes provide the spur needed to embrace new business practices and develop successful environmental strategies.

Introduction

In October 2005, Walmart's world headquarters in Bentonville, Arkansas, announced that the company would pursue a set of sweeping, long-term sustainability goals.[1] These aspirations included sourcing 100 percent renewable energy, creating zero waste, and selling products that sustain the environment.[2] Walmart intended for these changes to apply at all of its companies worldwide, including at Walmart Mexico.

After a slow start, Walmart Mexico has taken up the charge from Bentonville and made sustainability a major strategic priority. This effort has transformed the company into one of the world's most sustainable retailers, strengthened its brand, blunted government hostility, and protected Walmart's market position. Rather than adding financial burden, the company has found that sustainability actually *bolsters* its famous value proposition of "everyday low prices," while also achieving a heightened level of corporate social responsibility.

The Call to Action

Walmart's chain of stores and supercenters in Mexico emerged from a local entrepreneur's successful business empire. In 1958, Jerónimo Arango opened the Aurrera Bolívar market in Mexico City. Over the next three decades, Arango went on to build his umbrella company, Grupo Cifra, and established a network of retail and service stores under the Aurrera, Superama, Vips, and Suburbia brands. In 1997, Walmart bought Grupo Cifra, renaming the chain Walmart Mexico. After this acquisition, the retailer expanded rapidly throughout the nation.

Walmart Mexico now ranks as the largest Walmart company outside the United States and with more than 2,290 stores, it has become the largest retailer in Mexico. The company has traded on the Mexican Stock Exchange since 1977, originally as Grupo Cifra. In 2010, Walmart Mexico purchased Walmart Central America, adding 549 more locations across Guatemala, Honduras, El Salvador, Nicaragua, and Costa Rica. The company, now known as Walmart Mexico and Central America, commands a leading position in the Latin American retail sector.

The company has, however, faced some serious bumps on the road to success. Notably, in April 2012, the *New York Times* published an investigative report uncovering Walmart's history of corrupt practices in Mexico.[3] The Pulitzer Prize–winning story, titled "Vast Mexico Bribery Case Hushed Up by Wal-Mart After Top-Level Struggle," chronicled how Walmart representatives bribed government officials to obtain building permits as it expanded across Mexico. The report also questioned the accuracy and adequacy of the company's in-house investigation into corruption issues. Before the article's publication, the company had publicly downplayed the charges and prematurely ended an internal investigation. Walmart's in-house review had concluded that no clear evidence of bribery existed—a finding in direct conflict with later media reporting. In the company's commitment to rapid growth, Walmart executives in Mexico had failed to uphold the highest moral and ethical standards.

Guilty or not, Walmart suffered serious reputational damage from the corruption scandal, adding to widely discussed doubts about the social responsibility of the company's core business model.[4] On social issues, the company had already faced sharp criticism for years over its low wages, inadequate or nonexistent health care benefits, contentious labor relations, and emphasis on "big box" stores that pulled shoppers away from traditional downtowns. Environmentalist critics pointed to the company's long supply lines to loosely regulated production platforms in places like China. The company thus faced a business imperative: it had to recast its image in the eyes of its stakeholders without diminishing its value to shareholders. Fortunately for the company, it had already begun to deepen its commitment to sustainability, providing a foundation for rebuilding its reputation. In response to the corruption crisis, Walmart Mexico began to accelerate sustainability projects that had begun after the announcement seven years earlier in Bentonville.

Sustainability Analysis

On its website, the retail giant states, "At Walmart, we know that being an efficient and profitable business and being a good steward of the environment are goals that can work together." With this approach in mind, Walmart Mexico has implemented resource-saving technologies and processes. We now turn our focus to one particularly successful effort: Walmart Mexico has taken advantage of changes in the Mexican electricity market and invested in renewable energy. The company has managed to design and implement this portion of its corporate sustainability strategy while actually *reducing* operating expenses.

Walmart's Wind Farms

In many countries, wind farm developers struggle with regulations. In Mexico, these regulatory problems originate from the Constitution itself. According to the Mexican Federal Constitution, only the national utility company, the Comisión Federal de Electricidad, can sell power. Moreover, the utility must purchase power from the lowest-cost producer, ruling out the purchase of renewable power in most cases. These provisions have historically placed excessive burdens on aspiring wind farm developers. However, reforms in the electricity market starting in the mid-2000s enabled private companies, like Walmart, to step in. Under new provisions, electric grid users that took equity stakes in a power generation facility could "self-generate" electricity for their own use. Therefore, a company like Walmart could gain access to renewable energy resources by providing financing for an operator.

Internally, Walmart first tested this concept by looking at the financial calculus. Manuel Gómez Peña, the former director of sustainability at Walmart Mexico, explained in an interview that positive financial returns were a prerequisite to any investment.[5] After identifying that investments in wind power generators would actually reduce utility costs in the long term, Walmart began looking for a local shovel-ready partner. The company eventually signed a 15-year power purchase agreement with the La Ventosa wind farm run by Eléctrica del Valle de México (EVM). For the project to qualify under Mexico's self-generation regulations, Walmart Mexico purchased 0.8 percent of EVM's shares. With Walmart Mexico's power purchase agreement

in hand, the developers obtained additional external financing to purchase and erect wind turbines. Electricity generation began in 2010 for
348 Walmart facilities in central Mexico, representing 18 percent of the
company's electricity consumption. Walmart Mexico achieved multiple
goals with this project: the wind farm guaranteed *renewable* electricity,
and at rates 5–20 percent lower than existing prices. This first wind
power project spawned a broader corporate strategy of direct engagement with renewable energy providers.

Since starting to invest in renewable energy, Walmart Mexico has
participated in five wind farm projects: Eléctrica del Valle's La Ventosa
Wind Farm in Oaxaca, Électricité de France's Eoliatec del Istmo
Wind Farm and Eoliatec del Pacífico Wind Farm in the Isthmus of
Tehuantepec, Renovalia Energy and Desarrollos Eólicos Mexicanos's
Piedra Larga Wind Farm in Oaxaca, and Acciona Energía's Ingenio
in Oaxaca. These projects, along with one mini-hydroelectric plant,
generate more than 1,195 gigawatts per hour (GWh). This electricity powers 1,114 stores, offices, and distribution centers, representing
51 percent of the company's electricity needs. While the company's
renewable energy projects vary in scale, geography, and economic
return, all of them have helped to change perceptions about the company in local communities—and across the country.

Walmart Mexico's Sustainability Framework

Walmart Mexico has advanced corporate sustainability through its
wind farms, but the company is also pursuing broader environmental
goals. Today, Walmart Mexico's environmental policies ensure that
products and services minimize energy use, water consumption, waste,
air pollution, and biodiversity impact. To accomplish these goals,
Walmart Mexico's operation complies with both a set of internal company rules and government regulations, embraces a culture of continuous improvement, and promotes a culture of sustainability among
employees, suppliers, and customers.

In designing these rules, Walmart Mexico outlined five core sustainability goals. We have discussed Walmart Mexico's efforts to achieve

its energy goals, and the company has created separate initiatives to advance the other four goals:

1. *Energy*: Sourcing 50 percent of electricity needs from renewable energy.
2. *Waste*: Recycling or reusing 80 percent of residual materials generated by operations.
3. *Water*: Reusing 60 percent of the water used in stores.
4. *Products*: Expanding the supply of sustainable products.
5. *People*: Training and involving partners, particularly suppliers, in sustainability.

In 2012, as it worked to rehabilitate its reputation after the *New York Times* report, Walmart Mexico reported on its sustainability achievements over the previous ten years. The report highlighted the introduction of nearly 1,700 products with low environmental impact to the market. The company recycled 1,745 million kilograms of solid waste. Walmart Mexico also reported substantial progress on water conservation, with nearly 3 billion liters saved and 1.9 billion liters recycled in 774 water treatment plants.[6]

The company has also registered significant progress on energy use: By 2012, investments in energy had saved 420 million kilowatt hours of electricity through increased efficiency, in addition to generating 2,137 million kilowatt hours of renewable energy through the wind and hydroelectric projects described above. Direct renewable energy financing has played a substantial role in these achievements. These sustainability investments have also prevented the emission of 21,000 tons of carbon dioxide. According to Antonio Ocaranza, Walmart Mexico's director of corporate communications, the energy from these plants, along with other planned projects, will help achieve the goal of building a capacity of up to 3,000 GWh of renewable energy by the end of 2020.

Walmart embraces a strict business analytic approach to selecting its portfolio of renewable resources. In choosing between wind, solar, and hydro, Gómez Peña, the former director of sustainability at Walmart

Mexico, studied factors such as operational risk and required capital expenditure. He explained that all projects are monitored on an individual basis and that the company actively looks to obtain savings and avoid uncertainty in each phase of every project. Gómez Peña said that the company does not have a special evaluation basis for sustainability projects—instead, the company's investment group analyzes sustainability projects on the same basis as any other project, concentrating on the return on investment. In his role, Gómez Peña repeatedly confronted tensions between financial considerations and sustainability goals. He knew that gaining approval for investments required a demonstration of profitability, but felt in the long run "that trade-offs between economic development and environmentalism aren't necessary." After all, in his words, "the pursuit of sustainability can be a powerful path to reinvention for all businesses facing limits on their resources."[7] Ultimately, Walmart Mexico's success in sustainability found its roots with the company's existing corporate culture. In the renewable energy space in particular, financing new projects reduced costs and ultimately helped maintain the company's essential value proposition—low customer prices.

Conclusion

The sustainability strategy of Walmart Mexico emerged from the company's long-standing focus on lowering costs combined with a changing external environment. For the company to truly commit itself to implementing a sustainability strategy, executives had to prove financial viability. They also had to acknowledge the value of—indeed, the urgent need for—improved community engagement. Project managers analyzed new regulations, finding an opportunity to support struggling renewable energy developers and guaranteeing a cheaper, cleaner supply of electricity. In addition, the pressing need to improve the company's image refocused executives on opportunities that bolstered both corporate social responsibility *and* the bottom line.

Walmart Mexico's case offers several lessons for sustainability-aspiring companies. First, context remains important—the company's existing culture of operational efficiency aligned with new opportunities in the renewable energy market. Second, the right crisis—in this case over corruption—and the availability of shovel-ready projects helped push the retail company into a new sector. Renewable energy investment emerged as an essential tool for bolstering corporate social responsibility and improving operations. Sustainability actually came at a *profit*, and not a cost.

Chapter 3

GRUPO VANGUARDIA REVITALIZES PLASTICS RECYCLING IN HONDURAS

Felipe Perez and Martha Sofia Cifuentes

Abstract

Grupo Vanguardia, a Honduran plastics company, launched an innovative recycling initiative that has emerged as a core business strategy and foundation for marketplace success. This inclusive business model was built to reflect the economic realities of Honduras, a developing country with a struggling economy. By harnessing existing waste streams and a large base of previously informal workers, Grupo Vanguardia has delivered economic, environmental, and social gains in northeastern Honduras. The company has also gained higher margins by using recycled plastic, reducing waste, and creating jobs for low-income Hondurans. The Grupo Vanguardia case study demonstrates how sustainability can create opportunities for businesses in countries where the government is unable to provide essential services like waste management.

Introduction

Grupo Vanguardia, a Honduran plastics maker, has become a corporate sustainability pioneer. The company has developed a set of

---

This chapter builds on case #12161 "Grupo Vanguardia" (INCAE Business School, 2009), written by Jacky Rubio-Reyes, under the supervision of Felipe Perez. It has been written in collaboration with Sofia Moya (President, Grupo Vanguardia).

social and environmental practices that have given it a sustainability-driven competitive advantage. Vanguardia's success is especially notable because the plastics industry has long faced criticism for environmental damage and low recycling rates. The company's unique business model emerged from its engagement with local communities and commitment to helping Honduran society. Founder Eduardo Moya developed this guiding vision in partnership with the low-income informal workers who collect and recycle waste in northeastern Honduras. That collaboration, Moya learned, worked well. Indeed, after Grupo Vanguardia provided training and financial support, many of the individuals in the informal trash collecting sector were able to start formal businesses. The collectors' incomes increased, the company's bottom line improved, and discarded plastic was salvaged for successful reuse.

Grupo Vanguardia's Best Practice

Grupo Vanguardia has succeeded because it has developed a sustainable business model that reflects the realities of the Honduran economy. Honduras ranks among the poorest countries in Latin America, and informal work makes up a large share of the economy. Since its founding in 1992, Vanguardia has engaged with Hondurans to develop a new approach to plastic production. First, the company has taken advantage of the opportunity to use lower-cost recycled plastic as the feedstock for its manufacturing process, rather than relying on more expensive imported virgin plastic. Second, the company took on the opportunity to work with the working-class base of the Honduran social pyramid, folding the low-income trash collectors of the region, known as *pepenadores*, into its value chain. This new approach to business—combined with Eduardo Moya's passion for sustainability and social engagement—delivered more than just higher gross margins from recycled plastic. According to Grupo Vanguardia owners, by formalizing waste collectors' work, the company has created more than 1,300 indirect jobs that have benefitted at least 5,000 Hondurans.

Under this "inclusive" business model, Grupo Vanguardia has survived Honduran economic and political crises without losing money, and emerged as an influential player in the global plastics market. This chapter outlines Grupo Vanguardia's sustainability strategy with a focus first on the company's transition toward greater use of recycled materials. It then explores the implementation of the company's *inclusive* business strategy. Finally, it spells out the future challenges and policy implications of Grupo Vanguardia's approach.

Sustainability Strategy

Eduardo Moya initially founded Grupo Vanguardia's predecessor company, Plásticos Vanguardia, as a plastics manufacturer that relied solely on imported virgin materials. But after completing several corporate social responsibility trainings, Moya began to see the value of recapturing and reusing plastic waste. The challenge became a business opportunity, as Moya realized that acquiring recycled plastic would be 40 percent cheaper than using virgin materials.

Initially, the company focused on manufacturing a single finished product: plastic packaging for small juice containers. In 1992, the company had nine employees and processed 15,000 pounds of virgin plastic per month. When Moya decided to diversify production and sales in 1994, he founded two additional companies: ECOPLAST, focused solely on production from recycled materials; and ETICLASS, which produced adhesive labels. Those three companies, Plásticos Vanguardia, ECOPLAST, and ETICLASS, formed Grupo Vanguardia.

This new, expanded business model represented an opportunity for the business to grow while at the same time reducing plastic waste. To adopt it, however, Grupo Vanguardia needed to upgrade its machinery, change its operations, and rethink its culture. The company was making a big bet on sustainability—a bet that it might have lost.

Moya first had to invest in physical improvements to his production system, and decided to purchase a new recycling system from Austria. The company trained workers to operate this machinery, but more importantly, it also reoriented its corporate culture. The company redesigned its logo to reflect an environmental theme, and employees began collecting plastic in public areas. As noted above, the company began to rely on a broad network of previously informal trash collectors to create a new supply chain. Vanguardia formed a commercial alliance with a pilot group of collectors, and expanded the network by offering training, fair treatment, and reasonable purchase prices for recycled materials. This expanded supply chain helped Grupo Vanguardia establish new alliances with multinational companies in the textile and food industries and grew to represent 33 percent of its plastic sales in 2012.

Sustainability Analysis

Inclusive Business at Grupo Vanguardia

Grupo Vanguardia's inclusive business model evolved through the integration of plastic collectors into its value chain. The company recognized the importance of these collectors, most of whom worked in the informal economy, as a pathway to reduce costs *and* increase social benefits. As the partnership between collectors and the company deepened, managers sought to strengthen ties with the collector community through an explicitly inclusive approach. In fact, Grupo Vanguardia expressly aimed to help the collectors become micro-entrepreneurs. The company worked to expand the collectors' own supply networks by providing the training to hire employees and run a small business. Despite these opportunities, the company was entering into uncertain territory in building a new business model. The company would have to invest in building a new relationship with collectors in the hopes that the new approach would prove viable and allow for expanded waste recovery.

The collector engagement program developed in three phases, beginning in 2001. First, Grupo Vanguardia hosted a workshop for existing employees to craft its vision for collecting plastic. This employee engagement built a sense of ownership over the project. Next, the company formalized alliances, inviting a select group of clients, companies, and potential providers of recycled materials to the project launch event. This gathering would later form the core group for the collection initiative. Finally, Grupo Vanguardia began a pilot project to train 15 collectors, selected from a group of 124, based on the volume of recycled materials they collected and their willingness to participate. Subsequent workshops evaluated each collector's needs for managerial, administrative, technical, or financial support. In addition, the collectors learned about different types of plastics, the recycling process, business accounting, and regulatory issues facing manufacturers of recycled products.

Collectors began participating in the project largely because of the training and partnership opportunities with Grupo Vanguardia. The collection partnership reduced the uncertainty of working in the informal economy—a shift that fostered loyalty and commitment to Vanguardia. In interviews we conducted in 2012, collectors associated the program with words like "loyalty," "unity," "commitment," and "perseverance." When we asked about why the partnership has succeeded, they emphasized the respect that Grupo Vanguardia shows for all its stakeholders.

Through the pilot project, Grupo Vanguardia provided its collectors with the technical and managerial knowledge they needed to improve their productivity. During the pilot, the company came to understand the sustainability-driven marketplace advantage it had uncovered. It extended the project's timeline and added new collectors interested in participating. Grupo Vanguardia now works with 221 plastic providers, with nearly 5,000 people benefitting directly or indirectly from the 1,300 indirect jobs the partnerships have created.

Other Corporate Responsibility Initiatives

In 2010, as Grupo Vanguardia's collection partnerships grew, the company expanded its corporate social responsibility pillars to better reflect its evolving business model.[1] One of the new pillars, known as Plastic Providers, inspired a set of new initiatives to deepen Vanguardia's relationship with collectors. The first initiative was to expand the range of collector training sessions. These trainings began in 2008, expanding from purely plastics-related lessons to broader quality-of-life issues like personal health. The company educated collectors about preventing their exposure to disease during their work, and avoiding other conditions, such as HIV/AIDS, hepatitis, and tuberculosis. Over time, the company strengthened the training program by providing certifications to collectors who completed the sessions. The Plastic Providers pillar also led the company to offer incentives and support for the suppliers of recyclable materials. As part of this initiative, Grupo Vanguardia constructed a room at its headquarters in the city of San Pedro Sula dedicated to the collectors where they could wait while the accounting department processed payments. This modest investment sent the message that Grupo Vanguardia valued its partnership with collectors, typically a highly stigmatized segment of Honduran society. The company added to its engagement strategy by hanging a photo celebrating the "supplier of the month" in the collectors' room. Today, the suppliers that collect the most recyclable material receive prizes, with an annual awards ceremony honoring the top performers. Such activities help celebrate the success of the supply chain and strengthen ties between Grupo Vanguardia and its collectors.

Grupo Vanguardia's second new strategic pillar focused on public engagement. The company formed a partnership with the municipality of San Pedro Sula to expand its support system for collectors of recyclable materials. The company also established alliances with member companies of the Honduran Foundation for Corporate Social Responsibility (FUNDAHRSE) and helped create a national association for recyclers, the *Asociación Nacional de Gestores y Recicladores de Honduras*, to accredit participating firms and lobby for improved labor protections for informal workers. Grupo Vanguardia has won FUNDAHRSE's annual Socially Responsible Business Award eight times. This recognition underscores the company's transformation from an inwardly focused organization to one leading a society-wide transformation in business practices.

Drivers of Grupo Vanguardia's Success

The risk Grupo Vanguardia undertook with its alternative business model has borne fruit. Its production arm has processed 124.9 million pounds of recycled plastics. Grupo Vanguardia has posted monthly sales of over US$1.5 million, with 41 percent of sales coming from recycled plastic in 2017. The company continues to benefit from the high margins unlocked by converting plastic waste into new products.

Grupo Vanguardia achieved this success by innovating to avoid bottlenecks in its business model, following the "Value Proposition Canvas" approach developed by business guru Alex Osterwalder.[2] The company established key partnerships with collectors and invested in important resources (such as specialized equipment for recycled plastic production). It also allowed for more variable costs in its cost structure, recognizing that payments to collectors fluctuate based on their production and the market price for recycled plastic.

The company's environmental strategy has also evolved.[3] Initially, Grupo Vanguardia simply complied with Honduran environmental laws, no matter how lax the standard. But soon the company adopted a "beyond compliance" strategy and began to use its new environmental initiatives as a competitive advantage. The decision to focus on recycled plastic inputs changed the firm's internal culture and built awareness about the social benefits of recycling plastic. The company's engagement with civil society and the public sector helped invigorate Honduran corporate social responsibility and sustainability efforts.

While Grupo Vanguardia has profited from its environmentally friendly practices like waste reduction, it would be wrong to see its sustainability work as simply an all-upside approach. Expanding waste reuse through relationship-building with informal collectors was an unproven strategy with no guarantee of success. But through this effort, Grupo Vanguardia has achieved triple bottom line results: delivering economic, environmental, and social benefits for its community.[4] The inclusive recycling model has increased profitability, reduced environmental damage, and improved the livelihoods of low-wage, informal workers.

Potential Threats to Grupo Vanguardia's Sustainability Approach

Although Grupo Vanguardia has achieved several of its business objectives, challenges lie ahead. The company did not reach its 2016 growth goals and must now determine how to continue its historical success.

It has begun the search for new untapped *green* niches. For example, the company may expand into higher value-added products, such as "plastic lumber" and recycled bricks, to further diversify its product line and target more affluent customers. An expansion into international markets may also reinforce the company's growth. However, the company must first figure out how to manage increased competition for recycled materials within the country.

The broader Honduran context, unfortunately, also remains relevant. Honduras suffers from rampant violence and widespread gang activity. Some companies that once provided Grupo Vanguardia with plastic waste have left the country due to the security situation and unpredictable political climate. Although difficult economic times in Honduras have led more people to turn to waste collection—potentially benefitting Grupo Vanguardia—gangs may also begin to intrude on informal collection operations.

Conclusion

Grupo Vanguardia's inclusive, environmentally friendly business model provides a roadmap that may be applicable for businesses in many developing countries. The company has supported informal workers while also reducing the Honduran plastic industry's environmental impacts. (It may also be worth noting that part of the company's success may hinge on the fact that Honduras is poor, and thus provides a steady supply of both labor and raw material.)

Nonetheless, Grupo Vanguardia has succeeded in forging a network that a competitor would find difficult to replicate. In response to other companies tapping into the informal plastic waste stream, Grupo Vanguardia has provided loans to suppliers to increase their working capital at no extra financial cost. To further assist its suppliers, the company also actively searches for new businesses generating recyclable waste. Grupo Vanguardia has offered to handle the waste produced by these new businesses in partnership with their collectors. These efforts help to ensure the company's continued success as the Honduran market evolves.

Table 3.1 Plastic collectors by range of collection, 2009–15

Range (lb/mo)	2009	2010	2011	2012	2013	2014	2015
<= 1,500	76	110	143	151	171	149	155
1,501–3,000	11	13	17	17	20	24	23
3,001–4,500	10	15	7	7	10	10	12
4,501–6,000	6	8	6	7	8	7	10
6,001–7,500	2	6	4	5	5	7	4
7,501–10,000	2	4	3	4	6	7	6
10,001–15,000	8	9	3	5	6	5	6
15,001–20,000	4	5	2	2	2	3	2
> 20,001	5	3	4	5	2	2	4
Total	124	173	189	203	230	214	221

Source: Grupo Vanguardia.

Grupo Vanguardia's best practices—engaging in recycling and incorporating informal workers into its value chain—have significant policy implications. As collectors become suppliers and move into the formal economy, these individuals become potential taxpayers, generating more revenue for the Honduran government. The company's recycling practices simultaneously reduce the burden on government services. In this case, a private firm has decreased the amount of trash left in public places and supported working people entering the formal economy. These public benefits, usually considered the responsibility of the government, have nonetheless improved Grupo Vanguardia's bottom line.

Fundamentally, Grupo Vanguardia has demonstrated the potential to "create shared value" that benefits both the company and society.[5] Its innovative business model, tailored to local circumstances, has reduced environmental burdens in the communities where it operates, produced employment (Table 3.1) and economic gains at the base of the Honduran social pyramid, and generated continued profits for the company.

Chapter 4

NISSAN MEXICANA'S RENEWABLE POWER PARTNERSHIP

Aideé Figueroa López and Isidro Marco
A. Cristobal-Vazquez

Abstract

As part of its mission statement, Nissan Motor Corporation instituted the Nissan Green Program (NGP), a roadmap for making the Japanese automaker the worldwide leader in zero-emission mobility. In 2011, Nissan launched NGP 2016, the third iteration of its green program, focused on reducing its carbon footprint, shifting to renewable energy, and diversifying the resources the company uses. In keeping with NGP 2016, Nissan Mexicana—the company's Mexican subsidiary—took a risk by adopting renewable power for the largest of its three plants, located in Aguascalientes. Before 2012, the main source of electricity in Mexico was the government-backed Comisión Federal de Electricidad (CFE), which used mostly fossil fuels to produce power. Nissan's facility, known as Aguascalientes 1 (or A1), has been using electricity generated from biogas and wind since that time and, by 2014, obtained nearly half of its electricity from renewables. These renewable energy sources have saved Nissan Mexicana money, lowered greenhouse gas emissions, and bolstered the company's reputation. This chapter shows how Nissan Mexicana and its energy development partner, ENER-G, worked with municipal and state governments to match interests and enhance environmental sustainability.

Introduction

Climate change has deeply impacted the global automotive industry.[1] For nearly a century, the industry's main product—four-wheeled transportation powered by fossil fuel combustion—has been a major emitter of greenhouse gases (GHGs). Now, however, the tables have turned. The so-called carbon constraints to limit climate change are present in all automotive markets. These rules require auto manufacturers in the United States, European Union, and Japan to lower the carbon emissions of new vehicles and develop new technologies to help meet constraints. For example, according to Nissan's 2012 sustainability report, Japan's 2009 Emission Standards require a 47 percent reduction in nitrous oxide and 64 percent reduction in particulate matter emissions from 2005 levels for many Japanese vehicles.[2] Europe's 2015 "Euro 6" standard aims to reduce automotive emissions in graduated stages. All mass-produced automobiles and vans must now meet emissions standards for nitrogen oxide, carbon monoxide, hydrocarbons, and particulate matter.

Carbon constraints generate both risks and opportunities for manufacturers like Nissan.[3] Though new rules may be forcing automakers to change their practices, companies that use carbon constraints to drive innovation are creating competitive advantages. These carbon constraints pushed Nissan to develop the LEAF, now the most popular all-electric vehicle worldwide, according to the company. The LEAF is sold in 40 countries and has made Nissan the leader in this niche market.

Not wanting to be left in Nissan's dust, other major automakers have also expanded their environmental initiatives. These efforts include green buildings, eco-friendly design, green supply chains, green manufacturing, reverse logistics, the use of lightweight materials, increases in fuel efficiency, diversification of sources, reduction or removal of volatile organic compounds (VOCs), and the design of "smart" navigational systems to reduce traffic congestion.[4] According to experts, design is the key to countering environmental problems caused by the automotive industry across the entire life cycle of the product. Eighty percent of the negative environmental impact of a vehicle occurs out on the open road.[5]

The importance of design, in turn, is driving Nissan to be the leader for zero-emission mobility. To accomplish this noble but daunting goal, Nissan has been challenged to make fundamental changes in its business model, its processes, and even its products. Further, based on materiality assessment of management risk factors, Nissan has identified at least ten pressing environmental issues that automakers need to tackle. To address these issues, Nissan has defined an environmental strategy that aims to comply with regulations and meet stakeholder expectations, and at the same time, to raise global market share and profit margins. Thus, Nissan has advanced beyond merely stating a commitment to the environment and adhering to the letter of established laws; it has forged ahead into areas that are not mandated by law, such as eco-design.

Nissan's Best Practice

In Mexico, Nissan Mexicana S.A de C.V. (Nissan Mexicana) has focused on pollution control, pollution prevention, and eco-efficiency. One best practice that has emerged from this work is clean energy adoption. That is, Nissan Mexicana has tapped into energy sources that have until recently been ignored by the Mexican federal government. For generations, most electricity in Mexico has been produced and sold by the government-backed Comisión Federal de Electricidad (CFE), which relies on fossil fuels for 80 percent of its inputs. Alternative energy sources have allowed Nissan Mexicana to bypass the old, dirty energy paradigm long before other companies. The alternative energy sources have turned out to cost less money, while generating lower GHG emissions and bolstering Nissan Mexicana's brand value. Today, the company's plants have set the benchmark for Nissan facilities worldwide due to one remarkable achievement: *According to managers, they have the lowest electricity cost per vehicle manufactured of any Nissan plant worldwide.*

Taking a risk by breaking from the old CFE-only paradigm, Nissan Mexicana was one of the pioneers in developing a new way forward for other manufacturers in Mexico. The government has recently followed the lead of Nissan Mexicana and other pioneers by instituting reforms that allow private companies to participate more broadly in the power market. Here, then, is an example where the private sector led the way and policymakers followed.

This chapter lays out the role of Nissan Mexicana in the global auto industry, explains the company's sustainability strategy, and highlights how it has been able to produce energy from biogas generated in the main landfill of the state of Aguascalientes, in south-central Mexico. This bioelectricity provides the dual environmental benefit of displacing fossil fuels while also reducing methane production from the decomposition of organic waste. Nissan Mexicana made biogas energy a reality through its strategic partnership with local government and ENER-G, a private developer.

The Auto Industry in Mexico

According to the International Organization of Motor Vehicle Manufacturers (OICA), 94.9 million motor vehicles were produced globally in 2016, an increase of 8 percent over 2013, and a total increase of 18 percent over the previous five years. There were 1.236 billion vehicles in use around the world in 2014, an increase of 16 percent over the previous five years.

Mexico produced 3.46 million cars and light vehicles in 2016, of which 20 percent were for the domestic market and 80 percent for export. The main destination of exported vehicles was the United States (77 percent), followed by Canada (8.9 percent) and Latin America (7.3 percent). Mexican vehicles accounted for 12.2 percent of total US sales in 2016, and Mexico ranked as the top vehicle producer in Latin America and the seventh-largest worldwide. Nissan Mexicana manufactured one-quarter of all vehicles produced in the country, and the company was the largest producer of cars and light vehicles in Mexico in 2015.

In 2015, the Mexican auto sector made up 3 percent of national GDP and 18 percent of manufacturing GDP, and it was the source of 870,000 direct jobs.[6] As of 2017, ten global vehicle manufacturers have assembly facilities in Mexico.

Table 4.1 Nissan in Mexico

	Opened	Employees*	Vehicles produced (2014)
Regional office and R&D		1,438	
Aguascalientes 1 Plant (AGS1)	December 1982	7,292	377,969
Aguascalientes 2 Plant (AGS2)	November 2013	1,330	174,474
Cuernavaca Plant	May 1966	4,444	254,699
		14,504	807,142

Source: NISSAN Motor Corporation Fact File 2015.

* April 2014 through March 2015, excluding non-permanent workers.

Nissan Mexicana S.A. de C.V.

Nissan Motor Co. first came to Mexico in 1959 and established Nissan Mexicana S.A. de C.V. a year later, mainly to distribute the Datsun brand.[7] In 1966, its Cuernavaca plant began operations, 55 miles south of Mexico City and the first Nissan plant outside Japan. The first Aguascalientes plant, A1, began operations in 1982 as a US$1.3 billion investment. Aguascalientes plant A2 opened in 2013, and together with A1 produces 550,000 vehicles a year. Table 4.1 portrays Nissan's facilities in Mexico. In 2014, Nissan's all-electric vehicle, the LEAF, was released to the Mexican market. By 2015, the company had produced 500,000 vehicles with renewable energy sources and was, for six consecutive years, the car sales leader in Mexico.

In all, Nissan has a total yearly world production capacity of more than five million cars and light vehicles. Mexico is the company's fourth largest producer, after China, Japan, and the United States. The company plans to continue expanding in North America, with Mexico as a strategic hub. Nissan, through an alliance with Daimler and Renault, recently announced an investment of US$1 billion to develop a third manufacturing plant in Aguascalientes (A3) that will produce Mercedes-Benz and Infiniti vehicles.[8] The plant's annual capacity is estimated at over 300,000 vehicles by 2020, and this expansion is expected to create approximately 5,700 jobs.

Sustainability Strategy

Companywide, Nissan operates under the "Nissan Power 88" strategic plan to improve global market share and profit margins. Six strategies form Nissan Power 88: strengthening brand power, enhancing sales power, enhancing quality, business expansion, cost leadership, and zero-emission leadership.[9]

"The automotive industry is affected globally by various regulations and requirements related to the environment, such as exhaust emissions, GHGs, energy, fuel efficiency, noise, materials/recycling, water, hazardous substances, wastes, and these are becoming more stringent year by year," the company concluded in its 2014 Sustainability Report.[10] Nissan's environmental strategy aims to comply with those regulations and meet the expectations of its stakeholders. Stakeholders are most concerned about fuel consumption and sustainable mobility, including zero emissions, safety, quality, economic sustainability, renewable energy, air quality, water scarcity, carbon dioxide emissions in the manufacturing process, and resource efficiency.

Nissan has prioritized these issues accordingly. In 2011, the company created the Nissan Green Program 2016 (NGP2016). NGP2016 focuses on zero-emission vehicle penetration, fuel-efficient vehicle expansion, reducing new natural resource use, and minimizing carbon footprint, according to Nissan.[11] The company expects carbon dioxide emissions from production and business operations to peak in the 2020s.[12] To achieve these goals, the company is relying on four key pathways: the launch of the Nissan LEAF, which emits 40 percent less carbon dioxide than comparable gas vehicles; the development of improved fuel-efficiency technologies to enhance vehicle fuel efficiency by an average of 35 percent; a 25 percent increase in the use of recycled material; and a 20 percent decline in carbon emissions compared to 2005 levels.

Nissan Mexicana has been able to tailor NGP2016 to take advantage of local opportunities. The company has focused its manufacturing on pollution control and eco-efficiency. To minimize the use of natural resources, the company's main strategies are efficient water use and application of a 3R (reduce-reuse-recycle) philosophy for all in-house processes. The company has had a number of other environmental successes in Mexico as well. The Aguascalientes A1 facility has, since 2011, recycled 100 percent of its manufacturing waste. A1 and A2 installed a water treatment plant designed to discharge zero wastewater.

In logistics operations, the company has minimized its packaging, used reusable packaging where possible, and investigated the most efficient travel routes. Nissan Mexicana works to extend these practices to its suppliers through environmental trainings. The company's environmental management system includes performance indicators, employee training programs, internal and external environmental audits, and an Environment and Safety Manager position whose top responsibility is to deal with environmental issues. The A1 plant has also been ISO 14000 certified since 2001.

Nissan Mexicana's greatest environmental achievement is its energy use. The Mexican plants have achieved the lowest electricity cost per vehicle manufactured anywhere in the company. Nissan Mexicana Aguascalientes A1's energy systems are considered a best energy practice among all Nissan facilities worldwide. Nissan Mexicana has adopted renewable wind and biogas, as well as natural gas, that constitute competitive alternatives to the government-backed power utility CFE. These technologies create competitive advantages through lower cost and GHG emissions. This alternative energy effort does not come without disadvantages though, like intermittent service and little flexibility on consumption rates. However, Nissan Mexicana is able to toggle between these energy sources, thereby maximizing its environmental and economic benefit.

The Aguascalientes A1 plant is particularly noteworthy for its energy sourcing. In January 2012, the A1 plant began to use 1.4 megawatts (MW) of biogas energy produced by the main landfill in the state of Aguascalientes. Today, the biogas plant has a capacity of 2.5 MW and Nissan is its only end-user. In January 2013, the A1 plant also began to use 22 MW of wind-generated power. This energy is supplied by ENEL, a private electricity developer, from a wind farm located in Oaxaca, 590 miles from Aguascalientes City. The wind farm has 35 turbines with a capacity of 254,000 kilowatt-hours (kW-h) per year, and Nissan A1 has been using 192,000 kW-h on its assembly line. According to Nissan Mexicana, these initiatives made A1 the first Nissan facility in the world fully powered by renewable energy, accounting for 40 percent of the total renewable energy used globally by Nissan.

Sustainability Analysis: Biogas at Nissan Mexicana

Today, two-thirds of all global electricity is generated from fossil fuels, which are responsible for more than 40 percent of global energy sector-related carbon dioxide emissions.[13] In Mexico, the main supplier of electricity is the government-run CFE, whose energy matrix is made up of 80 percent fossil fuels.[14]

In this section, we explain how Nissan Mexicana has used biogas to help reduce its GHG emissions. Renewable electricity from sources like biogas has been incentivized in some countries with policy instruments such as feed-in tariffs, quotas, or auction systems.[15] However, in Mexico, despite a lack of financial incentives for renewable electricity, the CFE's electric rates for industrial and commercial consumers are high enough that some renewable power technologies can compete without subsidies. But the company remains at risk in a rapidly changing Mexican electricity market—and the long-term success of its renewable energy venture remains uncertain.

The Nissan Mexicana biogas project came about as a result of structural changes in the local, national, and international marketplaces. In short, a vast waste management problem in Aguascalientes—what to do with the trash of a sprawling city of one million residents?—was solved by turning to private renewable energy entrepreneurs. Table 4.2 portrays the path that this project followed.

After Aguascalientes City tripled its land base from 3,262 hectares to nearly 8,600 between 1980 and 2010 and doubled its population, waste generation surpassed the capacity of the municipally controlled "Las Cumbres" dump. It was forced to close operations in 1998. The municipal government decided to build a landfill in the "San Nicolas" zone, northwest of the city.

Table 4.2 Chronology of events affecting the Nissan Mexicana Biogas Project

Year	Condition	Action	Leader	Outcomes
1998	Waste generation surpassed the capacity of former dump	Built a new landfill	Aguascalientes municipality	Waste Management Strategy
2005	NOM-083 Regulation (the biogas control requirement)	Construction of the biogas collection and destruction system	Municipality and ENER-G	Compliance with regulation
2006	CDM funding opportunity	Registration of the project under CDM	Municipality and ENER-G	Obtain revenues (ENER-G) and royalties (municipality) by selling carbon credits (CERs)
2008	Global financial crash (carbon prices fell)	Stop to sale of carbon credits	Municipality and ENER-G	Stopped getting revenues and royalties
2008	Energy Law reform (private companies can generate electricity) and high CFE rates for big users	Analyze electricity generation opportunity	ENER-G	Bioelectricity generation project
2008	Common interest to manage social, environmental, and financial performance simultaneously	Made an agreement	Municipality, ENER-G, and Nissan Partnership = SAEVA	Renewable power strategy

Once the management of waste was addressed, in January 2005, the Aguascalientes City Council invited several companies to present project proposals for the collection and destruction of biogas in the Las Cumbres dump and San Nicolas landfill. The Mexican regulation NOM-083 SEMARNAT states that the biogas generated in landfills should be controlled and burned, or used for alternative purposes. In November, Biogas Technology LTD—an ENER-G sister company— and the municipality of Aguascalientes signed an agreement for the collection and destruction of biogas at both sites. The agreement stipulated that ENER-G was responsible for financing the biogas collection and its destruction.

This project was then registered under the Kyoto Protocol's Clean Development Mechanism (CDM) in July 2006, which allowed it to obtain revenues by selling carbon credits. These revenues should have covered operation costs, royalties to the municipality, and profits for the investor. However, after the global financial crash in 2008, carbon prices fell dramatically, therefore, sales of carbon credits fell short of expected revenues. Biogas Technology LTD was unable to pay Aguascalientes and ENER-G's investors.

All was not lost, however. New rules from Mexico's Energy Law reform in 2008, as well as the high cost of electricity from the state-run CFE, created new opportunities for private companies to sell power at a more competitive price. Because Nissan Mexicana had shown interest in a renewable power project, ENER-G sought to partner with the automaker. All factors were taken into consideration: economic feasibility, biogas availability, and potential end-users.

In Mexico, the federal government still owns most electricity generation capacity. However, the energy reform law has yielded opportunities to privately generate electricity through self-supply (or *auto-abastecimiento*), in which the end-user can buy electricity produced by a private developer if the end-user has a nominal investment in the energy producer (and thus qualifies as "owner"). The price is negotiated between the private producer and the end-user—in this case, ENER-G and Nissan Mexicana. The power moves through the government-monitored electric grid by paying a transport tariff. An end-user or off-taker can be a municipality, industry or other commercial enterprise. To minimize risk and make the arrangement profitable, private energy developers such as ENER-G typically seek credit-worthy off-takers with stable consumption patterns.

Nissan Mexicana's Motivation

When changes in Mexican law allowed private companies to generate power, none of the players—producers, off-takers, government officials—were certain of the rules. In this context, Nissan's foray into renewable energy was an ambitious and potentially risky undertaking. Pioneers who could navigate the new terrain emerged, including Marco Ribera, Environment and Safety Manager at Nissan Mexicana. At that time, there was a dearth of independent power projects. Ribera and former executives of EcoSecurities, a company associated with ENER-G that began to promote CDM projects in Mexico, talked about possible power generation in the Aguascalientes landfill, where ENER-G was already developing the biogas collection and destruction system. The idea was appealing to Ribera but it needed further study because of the lingering uncertainty in the new marketplace.

Nissan Mexicana's first experiment with the energy market beyond the CFE was with a thermoelectric plant. The company's motivation was partly driven by a need for cheaper power. As the partnership progressed, fears arose within Nissan Mexicana management that becoming an investor in another private enterprise would detract from its core business and require more responsibility than simply making cars. Then there was the matter of the Power Purchase Agreement (PPA), which bound Nissan Mexicana to be the consumer of all the electricity generated. Concern also grew at Nissan headquarters in Japan over this arrangement, unprecedented for any automaker. But in the end, the generally positive results of the thermoelectric project justified the risks and allayed fears throughout the company. When the PPA term was completed, Ribera began looking for other renewable energy sources.

Because Nissan Mexicana is recognized as an important economic development driver in the Aguascalientes region, the municipal government and ENER-G were ready to facilitate a more lasting relationship. At Nissan headquarters in Japan, the Aguascalientes complex is seen as a strategic location for growth in the Americas. After carbon prices fell, ENER-G and Aguascalientes realized that Nissan Mexicana was a desirable off-taker. The company, in turn, saw this as an opportunity to get electricity at a more competitive price and achieve its sustainability goals through the usage of bioelectricity. Because barriers within the company had fallen, Nissan Mexicana found the transition to biogas and wind power far easier than its earlier foray into thermo-electricity. The company also knew the government's requirements. So, after investing in ENER-G, Nissan Mexicana began construction of the power plant in August 2011. The plant was operational by March 2012.

Once the parties reached an agreement, a "vehicle" company was needed to take advantage of the self-supply mechanism. They formed SAEVA for this purpose, with ENER-G as owner of the biogas collection and power-generation equipment and Biogas Technology LTD as owner of the biogas rights. Nissan Mexicana is now only a minor partner. Nissan Mexicana and SAEVA signed a five-year power purchase agreement to supply 2.5 MW to the A1 facility. The agreement set a rate for electricity lower than the commercial CFE rate.

For Nissan Mexicana, becoming the off-taker of this renewable energy enables it to achieve an important environmental objective and add value through this cost-competitive source. Accordingly, Nissan Mexicana's vice president of manufacturing stated that "this project allows us four years to advance the environmental challenges of our Nissan Green Program 2016 to reduce [carbon dioxide] emissions; besides showing the value of working as a team to improve the environment."[16]

ENER-G's investment of US$7.1 million in its biogas project has paid off handsomely. The San Nicolas landfill receives a total of 1,000 tons per day of household, commercial, and industrial waste. The power plant at the 60-hectare site generates about 2.5 MW of electricity using 1,200 cubic meters per hour of methane gas from this waste material. The electricity is transported to Nissan's facility through overhead lines over a distance of 12.4 miles through a supply contract with the CFE. This project helps to reduce carbon dioxide emissions at the landfill site by nearly 90,000 tons per year.

Conclusion

Nissan Mexicana's renewable energy generation partnership illustrates a generalizable best practice. A local government owning and operating landfills can enter into partnerships with private power developers and private manufacturing companies to ensure that the maximum feasible amount of methane is recovered for renewable energy generation. This case demonstrates that beyond their economic interests, the entities all share environmental and social commitments, forming the basis for successful green partnerships.

Nissan relies on continuous improvement in all its business areas. Its environmental management system establishes mechanisms to motivate employees to improve outcomes. Nissan Mexicana's environment and safety manager and all employees who are involved in environmental issues take sustainability challenges seriously. When new rules were put in place to allow private companies to produce power, Marco Ribera saw the opportunity to tap into a green power source, and took the time necessary to make the new paradigm a success.

The success of this bioelectricity project and the lessons learned from it allowed Nissan Mexicana to adopt other types of clean energy. Today, renewable energies (biogas and wind) account for half of the electricity consumed in the A1 plant. Renewable sources and lower-carbon natural gas make up 90–95 percent of its energy consumption. This advantage represents approximately a benefit of 10 percent of total electricity cost for the A1 plant.

However, in Mexico an energy project is never risk free. In December 2016, the contract for electricity supply was due to be renegotiated. Since the alliance has met the expectations of all partners so far, the parties signed another five-year agreement, the maximum period Nissan allows for a contract of this type. However, the original agreement with Nissan set a rate for the electricity as a percentage of the commercial rate offered by CFE. In January 2012, the cost of one kilowatt-hour on intermediate time tariff was \$1.1721 MXN. But in January 2016, the kilowatt-hour at the same conditions was \$0.6757 MXN, which accounts for a 40 percent reduction in kilowatt-hour cost. CFE's reduced price is a threat to the continuation and expansion of renewable energy. Renewable energy investors and nongovernmental organizations have pointed out the need for the Mexican government to stop subsidizing electricity and recognize that there are additional costs to generating electricity from fossil fuels. Once these costs are codified by governmental action, clean energies can be developed more expansively.

The Aguascalientes municipality also represents a constant risk. In Mexico, the term in office for elected officials is three years, with the possibility of reelection. In spite of the fact that there is an agreement between the municipality and Biogas Technology LTD for biogas rights, a new government could potentially opt to stop this project. With a relationship built up over 30 years between the municipality and Nissan Mexicana, all of the key parties expect that the cooperation in this project will continue, but local politics constitute an enduring risk for Nissan's sustainability strategy.

As of our writing of this chapter, there was great uncertainty over the unclear trade policies of the new US government. Nissan Mexicana and its stakeholders in its energy partnership should be aware of three issues: the renegotiation of the North American Free Trade Agreement (NAFTA); the proposed 20 percent tariff on Mexican imports into the United States; and the US administration's skepticism toward anthropogenic climate change. This could be an advantageous mix of factors for the company but also a setback for its clean-energy program.

Chapter 5

TECNOSOL FOLLOWS THE SUN

Felipe Perez and Martha Sofia Cifuentes

Abstract

Tecnosol is a solar power company founded in Nicaragua in 1998, which now has twenty-one branches throughout Central America. The company has profitably responded to the high demand for electricity in a rural region suffering from energy poverty, and has brought electricity to over 500,000 Central Americans. It has pioneered the use of microcredit to offer quality solar products to customers in rural areas who would otherwise not be able to afford them. Tecnosol then follows up on each purchase by teaching customers how to maintain their solar products so that their investment pays for itself quickly. This chapter chronicles Tecnosol's founding in the aftermath of the Nicaraguan civil war and analyzes its expansion throughout Central America. It then breaks down how Tecnosol attains results measurable at the triple bottom line—economic, environmental, social—demonstrating how sustainability can be a profitable business strategy, even in communities with low purchasing power.

Introduction

Tecnosol, a solar power company in Nicaragua, was founded in 1998 by Vladimir Delagneau, a Nicaraguan soldier who learned about solar

---

This chapter builds on case #12343 "Tecnosol" (INCAE Business School, 2012), written by Jorge Luis Carrion Saavedra, under the supervision of Felipe Perez. It has been written in collaboration with Vladimir Delagneau (founder and CEO, Tecnosol).

power during the country's civil war in the 1980s. In founding Tecnosol, Delagneau was able to transcend the limitations of state regulations, contribute to Nicaragua's socioeconomic development, and enhance environmental protection. Driven by its founder's commitment to sustainability, Tecnosol has responded to an untapped market for clean energy in northern Nicaragua. By continually updating its position in the solar power field, the company has expanded; it now has 21 branches, covering rural and urban markets in Nicaragua and throughout Central America.

Tecnosol's success shows it is possible to do profitable business in a region characterized by energy and fuel scarcity. By selling and installing solar panels, Tecnosol offers customers in Central America an off-the-grid, environmentally friendly energy solution, transforming the quality of life and economic productivity of rural residents. Today, the renewable energy company continues to operate successfully in areas where access to electricity is limited and power is expensive, as well as areas that lack institutional frameworks to encourage clean energy. Not limited to rural markets, however, Tecnosol has also brought clean energy to the urban market, where electricity is even more expensive and environmentally destructive. Tecnosol now offers a wide range of products and services through an integrated value chain (see Figure 5.1 and Table 5.1) powered by solar energy: from importing materials to sales, installations, and maintenance.

Tecnosol's achievements have been driven by a range of factors, including Delagneau's commitment to sustainable development, the region's unmet demand for electricity, Nicaragua's energy poverty, the microfinance and international financial institutions in place, and the increased efficiency and affordability of solar energy technology.

Tecnosol's Best Practices

Tecnosol has used an innovative business model that offers microcredit. This financing structure has allowed the company to work with the base of the social pyramid through indirect employment of product distributors. In addition, microcredit has allowed Tecnosol to

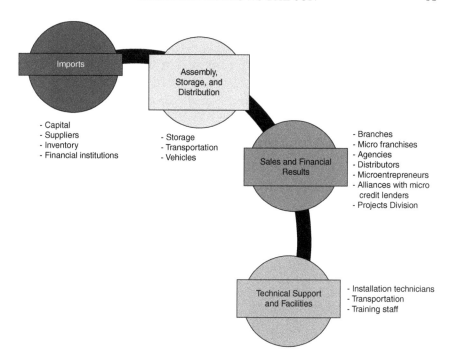

Figure 5.1 Tecnosol's simple business model.

greatly expand its pool of potential customers by giving low-income Nicaraguans the ability to purchase solar panels.

Tecnosol also offers high-quality products, covers diverse electrical needs beyond simply lighting, and delivers at the triple bottom line (social, environmental, economic). This chapter situates Tecnosol within a wider conversation about corporate sustainability, describes the firm's sustainability strategy, and highlights the company's environmental strengths. We then discuss Tecnosol's evolution from its origins, its future challenges, and the policy implications of its business model.

Tecnosol's Roots

In 1986 Vladimir Delagneau, then 18 years old, was conscripted into military service and transferred to Mulukukú, a remote community in the North Atlantic Region of Nicaragua. Delagneau recalled, "They told me I was going to go fight the 'Contra' with my knowledge,"

Table 5.1 Comparative view of Central America, 2015

	Panama	Costa Rica	El Salvador	Honduras	Nicaragua	Guatemala
Population (millions of inhabitants)	3.9	4.8	6.1	8.1	6.1	16.3
Territory (km²)	74,340	51,060	20,720	111,890	120,340	107,160
GDP per capita (PPP in US$)	20,885	14,647	8,096	4,785	4,884	7,253
Population density (inhabitants/km²)	52	94	296	72	50	153
% living below national poverty line*	23.0	21.7	31.8	62.8	29.6	59.3
% in urban areas	67	77	67	55	59	52
% in rural areas	33	23	33	45	41	48
HDI position	60	69	116	131	125	128
EPI Index Rank, 2016	51	42	97	89	115	88

Source: Human Development Index (HDI), Millennium Development Goals Database, World Development Indicators Database, Environmental Performance Index (EPI).

*Values for El Salvador, Honduras, Nicaragua and Guatemala as reported in 2014.

referring to the Contra rebels at war with Nicaragua's Sandinista government. Indeed, because of his knowledge in electronics, his duty was to identify the frequencies used by insurgent radios. His "headquarters" was a house on top of a hill. This house provided Delagneau's first exposure to life without electricity. In an interview from 2012, Delagneau recounted:

> At six o clock, I would go downhill to have dinner in town. I would eat with the locals and I experienced what people who lived in this area had to deal with on a daily basis: breathing air from wood fires or kerosene which people used for lighting and cooking, not being able to distinguish people's faces when having dinner, having to eat without seeing what's on one's own plate. Afterwards, when dinner was over, I had to go back to work and deal with the excessive smoke and nauseating smell of gasoline from the power generator that I needed in order to be able to see and operate my assigned communication radios.[1]

After six months in Mulukukú, Delagneau received a solar panel from an army soldier who had rescued it during an encounter with the Contras. Despite having no experience with solar power, Delagneau quickly had the panel functioning. From that moment, he became attracted to the benefits the technology could bring to communities with little or no electricity. One year later, Delagneau was transferred (without his solar panel) to another small village, Wiwilí, on Nicaragua's northern border with Honduras. Here he had to climb a steep hill with five gallons of gasoline each day to operate the generator to power his radios.

Delagneau was moved by his experiences during the civil war. At the time, Nicaragua's energy situation was among the worst in Central America. In the late 1990s, the country's energy matrix was based almost entirely on imported fossil fuels. The cost of importing fossil fuels was exorbitant—equivalent to 70 percent of Nicaragua's total exports. Central America's 80 percent electrification rate also fell below the Latin American average of 90 percent (Figure 5.2).

Delagneau believed photovoltaic (PV) systems could be an inexpensive way to bring electricity to areas the national power grid had

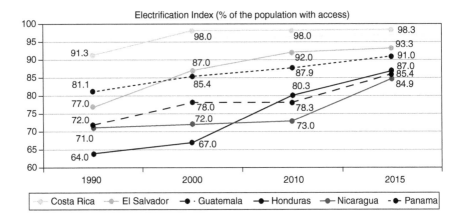

Figure 5.2 Electrification index in Central America.
Source: For 1990–2010, World Development Indicators; for 2015, Yale Environmental Performance Index 2016 Report.

yet to reach. In 1995, after the end of the war, Delagneau used his personal savings and a loan from his employer to purchase 15 PV systems for resale. Selling these systems was no simple task, though. Delagneau's target market was located far from the Nicaraguan capital of Managua, where solar power was unfamiliar. He thus had to travel in his free time to educate potential customers. "At the beginning, people didn't believe that the sun could provide electricity for their houses," he said.

In 1998, Delagneau officially founded Tecnosol, and focused the company on supplying and installing PV systems in rural areas. These installations were almost all domestic solar systems (solar home systems, or SHSs), which are used to light homes, schools, businesses, and health centers. The solar home systems comprised a PV module that generated electricity from sunlight, a rechargeable battery that stored electricity for use at night and during cloudy days, a charge controller that stopped the battery from overcharging or from discharging in excess, light bulbs, cables, and accessories. Florescent and LED lights could be used interchangeably. These SHSs varied from 25 Watt peak (Wp) to 200 Wp, with an average size of 60Wp.[2] Tecnosol also sold phone chargers, televisions, DVD players, sound systems and radios, according to its customers' needs and means.

By 2001, Delagneau had devoted himself fully to Tecnosol, and the company joined the Increased Use of Renewable Energy Resources Program, known by its Spanish acronym FENERCA.[3] FENERCA provided entrepreneurs with the businesses skills and training needed to launch and grow clean-energy companies in the region. The program was financed by USAID and E+Co, a New Jersey–based nongovernmental organization (NGO) that made clean-energy investments in developing countries. During Tecnosol's participation in FENERCA, the company demonstrated its growth potential—if adequate financing could be made available. Delagneau recalled in an interview:

> Like any small business, one of our greatest problems was a lack of working capital, which made us incur many additional costs as we were only able to import small volumes of our products. On the other hand, since our target market was the base of the pyramid, many of our potential clients did not have the ability to pay us in full; the products we were offering cost between US$850 and US$3,000, which is why we partnered with microfinancing companies. However, in many rural areas of the country where there was no electricity, there were also no microfinancing companies. This led us to start thinking that we should be able to provide these micro-loans ourselves.

With this goal in mind E+Co gave the company a US$100,000 loan when the FENERCA program ended in 2003. The loan helped Tecnosol increase its inventory and expand its market. Crucially, it also gave Tecnosol the ability to provide micro-loans to its clients, as we describe in detail below. As part of the National Energy Commission's Rural Electrification Plan, launched with financial support from the Inter-American Development Bank (IDB) between 2003 and 2005, Tecnosol helped expand electric services to 1,422 households in the municipality of Waspam Río Coco, located in the Northern Atlantic Autonomous Region (RAAN) of Nicaragua. For the first time, 32 communities in Waspam Río Coco were able to access electricity.

Delagneau wanted to reach more rural communities, but with only one distribution office in Managua expansion would have been costly, and customer service difficult to provide. So in 2004,

Delagneau developed an expansion strategy and requested a new loan from E+Co. With an additional US$200,000, he expanded his operations and established new branches. Many of the IDB officials Delagneau had met during the Waspam Río Coco project were interested in Tecnosol's methodology, products, and services. Because lack of capital continued to be the company's greatest barrier, the IDB granted Tecnosol a US$520,000 loan and more than US$180,000 in technical cooperation. This assistance would allow Tecnosol to provide electricity to 900 households (with more than 4,500 people) in 15 rural communities in southern and central Nicaragua. With the extra capital, Tecnosol could be in charge of not only installation but also operational training for these systems, their maintenance, credit provision to customers, and the collection of micro-loan fees.

Given Tecnosol's track record, E+Co continued to provide additional loans to advance the company's expansion strategy. Between 2004 and 2010, these loans accounted for nearly US $2 million and allowed Tecnosol to open its central office in Managua and 17 branches in rural regions of Nicaragua with limited access to electricity. Then, starting in 2007, the CASEIF II[4] fund, which provides venture capital to growing Central American companies, invested US$1.15 million in Tecnosol, acquiring 20 percent of the company's shares. This investment allowed Tecnosol to begin expanding to other countries beyond Nicaragua, where not only electricity prices were high but also existed an unmet demand for electrification in rural areas.

Expanding beyond Borders

When he started Tecnosol, Delagneau planned to consolidate his operations in Nicaragua, then eventually expand into other Central American countries. This regional expansion began in 2009, when Tecnosol won the bid for the Millennium Challenge Corporation's FOMILENIO project to install 500 household PV systems in the northern zone of El Salvador. Because the winning contractor had to provide an inventory of spare parts to guarantee operation and maintenance of the PV systems for at least two years, Delagneau decided to open a Tecnosol branch in San Salvador, El Salvador's capital city. This branch enabled Tecnosol to provide maintenance services as well as enter El Salvador's market. As Delagneau recalled, "There was very little promotion and development of renewable energy, especially for household or community use in the country." This FOMILENIO project benefited the departments of La Unión, Cabañas, San Miguel, Morazán, and Chalatenango, and the SHS installations were concluded in July 2010.

The El Salvador project underscored Tecnosol's ability to quickly build large installations of PV systems in difficult-to-access remote areas. Consequently, Tecnosol won the bid for a Panama-based electrification project in the Kuna Yala archipelago and in the city of Colón, financed by the Panama Rural Electrification Office (OER) with funds from the IDB. The project required the installation of 1,075 PV systems distributed among 1,063 households, 10 schools, and 2 health centers. It took place from January to June 2011, with a total investment of US$1,740,000.

Tecnosol entered the Honduran market quite differently, through a private venture that had been formed before the company had been awarded any major projects. At the end of 2012, Tecnosol was given the World Bank's Phase II PROSOL project, installing more than 6,000 autonomous PV systems in remote communities. This financing gave beneficiaries subsidies of up to 50 percent on solar energy systems. In 2013, Tecnosol opened two more branches in Honduras and in 2016 it opened a second branch in Panama. By then, Tecnosol was operating in four countries, with fifteen branches in Nicaragua, three in Honduras, two in Panama, and one in El Salvador (see Figure 5.3). Although Delagneau wanted to continue his expansion, he realized further growth would require a change in strategy. Namely, adopting a franchise approach to reach countries like Colombia without all the risks of the company's previous expansion endeavors.

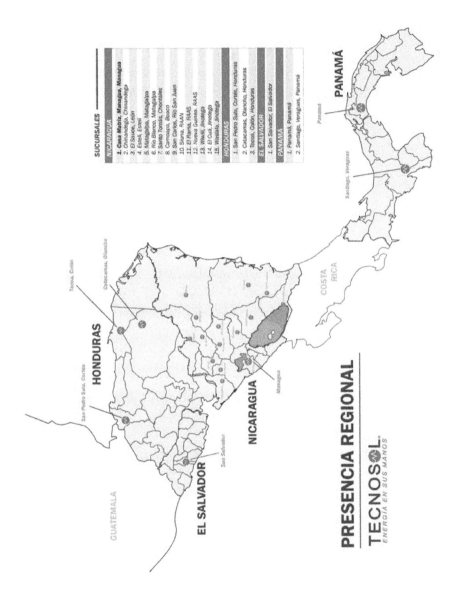

Figure 5.3 Regional presence of Tecnosol *sucursales*, or branches.
Source: Tecnosol.

Tecnosol's Strategy for Sustainable Business

In order to advance environmental sustainability and do business in rural, low-income regions of Central America, Tecnosol had to find innovative solutions to a number of unique challenges. The company operates in a region poor in conventional energy sources. Central America produces no natural gas, oil, or coal. While renewable energy sources such as wind, biomass, geothermal, and hydropower existed when the company was founded in 1998, they were difficult to develop due to financial, social, and environmental constraints. New opportunities began to appear, however, as PV solar panel systems became increasingly affordable, making solar power more accessible to low-income populations. Rising incomes, regional economic growth, and urbanization also drove this increase in accessibility.

Microcredit was also a central strategy for reaching Tecnosol's customer base. From the start, rural customers represented most of Tecnosol's business. In 2016, approximately 92 percent of Tecnosol's sales were to low-income customers with little or no education, living in rural areas far beyond the reach of conventional electricity services. Because the cost of solar equipment is beyond the means of most rural residents—for example, the company's most popular item costs US$1,120—Tecnosol decided to offer financing for each installation. It established partnerships with several microfinance firms and rural banks, and started its own in-house microcredit program for customers who did not obtain external financing.

To serve its customers, Tecnosol partners with several microfinancing institutions that grant Tecnosol's clients micro-loans to purchase solar home systems. But because many of the communities Tecnosol serves do not have access to these microfinancing institutions, the company also offers micro-loans directly to clients and takes responsibility for collecting loan payments. This service was made possible through company credit lines (obtained from local banks) and through Tecnosol's alliance with NGOs like Kiva, an American nonprofit with an online platform that connects lenders and borrowers all over the world. As customers repay their loans, Tecnosol keeps interest payments and sends Kiva the principal.

For large installations completed in alliance with governments or international institutions such as the IDB, Tecnosol is paid by the institution, which then works out a repayment plan with customers directly. In other cases where subsidies are involved, clients pay for the total minus the subsidy (for example, 80 percent of the product or service), and Tecnosol temporarily finances the remaining 20 percent until the project is completed. Upon completion, Tecnosol is paid the 20 percent by the institution, and the client obtains a product or service at the subsidized price.

Financing continues to be an area of deliberation as the initial costs of Tecnosol's products and services increase due to innovation and technology improvements. Balancing cost increases with Delagneau's desire to reach those most in need of his products and services has been a constant challenge.

Tecnosol's Inclusive Business Model

Delagneau's business model is characterized by low profit margins, high volume sales, and unconventional distribution channels. Because Tecnosol installed most of its early solar panels in remote communities but operated out of urban areas, post-sale services and repairs were costly (Table 5.2). The company therefore prioritized equipment delivery and installation, as well as customer service, which helped minimize the costs of equipment maintenance. Tecnosol also trained entrepreneurs from rural areas to become distributors and gave them inventory credit ranging from US$1,000 to US$5,000. Able to generate extra earnings by providing maintenance services to projects previously built by Tecnosol, these distributors became a key part of the company's low-cost model.

Today, Tecnosol has become known for its personalized, comprehensive customer service. The company not only installs solar home systems, it also trains clients in the correct use of these systems. Tecnosol provides maintenance services to all installed systems in the event of damage, increasing customer confidence.

Once sales are made, the most critical point in Tecnosol's business model is the company's installation service. Thus, the company makes

Table 5.2 Tecnosol's main products

Rural solutions (92% of income) by type of product (%)		Urban solutions (8% of income) by power demand range (%)	
Residential solar PV systems	70	Commerce (10 kW–50 kW)	45
Refrigeration systems	7.5	Industry (20 kW–5 MW)	25
Water pumping systems	5	Solar heaters	20
Peak energy systems	5	Urban homes (1 kW–10 kW)	10
Electric fences	2.5		
Chemical waste digester	2		
Other	8		

Source: Tecnosol.

sure to adequately train its installation technicians. The technicians are responsible for training customers to properly maintain their solar home systems and make simple repairs. Customer training is vital because Tecnosol has committed to all-inclusive customer service, and SHSs that are not well maintained or that customers can't repair would require technicians to return to client communities. In most cases, this would mean long, expensive trips to remote areas. In any case, post-installation costs for customers are low. Batteries last between five and six years, depending on usage, and their cost is approximately 30 percent of the entire system. Other than replacing their SHS batteries (obtained at a discounted price if customers return the old battery), clients have to make sure their PV panels are cleaned during the summer, a task that can also be performed by local technicians trained by Tecnosol.

Sustainability Analysis

Tecnosol has taken advantage of opportune timing and strategic partnerships in order to expand renewable energy access in Nicaragua. By 1998, the Nicaraguan government was able to muster enough political will to tackle the energy problem (further legislation supporting the energy sector passed in 2004), multilateral banks were willing to support renewable energy initiatives, solar panels had become more affordable due to the entry of Chinese manufacturers, and other marketable products like radios and DVD players could be imported,

further diversifying Tecnosol's portfolio. The state's traditional involve-
ment in the energy sector made government a natural ally.

After securing its reputation as a robust and reliable company with
technical expertise, Tecnosol has completed massive rural installations
either in alliance with governments or with funds from international
organizations like the World Bank. The results have borne out the
success of Tecnosol's business model: Within seven years of its
founding, Tecnosol was the solar power market leader in Nicaragua.
In 2016, Tecnosol had 115 employees and monthly sales ranging from
US$250,000 to US$440,000. Furthermore, between 2005 and 2011,
the company registered an average growth in sales of 40 percent per
year, which peaked at 70 percent in 2007.

Tecnosol's growth in Nicaragua has declined sharply in recent
years, for several reasons: the emphasis on financing projects in the
other Central American countries; the drop in solar panel prices; the
entry of new competitors offering cheaper panels into the market;
the nationwide increase in electrification; and the slowed growth of
the Nicaraguan economy due to the 2014–15 declines in the agricultural and livestock sectors, as well as a 2016 drought. (See Table 5.3 for
financial statements by country.)

Despite these challenges, Tecnosol has had a large impact on Central
American rural communities. By 2015, Tecnosol had installed more
than 95,000 solar-power PV systems throughout Central America,
benefitting more than 500,000 people. Families saved an estimated
US$340 per year, and Tecnosol systems prevented over 35,000 tons per
year of carbon dioxide emissions. In addition, families were better able
to engage in productive activities like business, agriculture, health, and
education. We explore these benefits in more detail in the "Tecnosol's
Impact" section.

Applying Alex Osterwalder's canvas model to Tecnosol,[5] we can see
that the firm innovated in the parts of the business where bottlenecks
appeared through key partnerships, customer relations, distribution
channels, and customer segments. Key partnerships with international
financial institutions have expanded Tecnosol's reach. The firm's
investment in customer relations has reaped rewards in an increasingly

Table 5.3 Tecnosol sales in 2015, by country and product

Product line	Nicaragua		Honduras		Panama		El Salvador	
	Total sales US$	% of total	Total sales US$	% of total	Total sales US$	% of total	Total sales US$	% of total
Rural SHS (panel, battery, controller, electric materials, installation)	3,631,300.53	**72.40**	1,329,335.89	**91.31**	183,962.39	**61.17**	152,630.12	**98.35**
Refrigerators	104,424.74	2.08	2,911.70	0.20	360.89	0.12	0.00	0.00
Water pumps	50,523.52	1.01	727.92	0.05	691.70	0.23	0.00	0.00
Biodigestors	12,249.66	0.24	1,164.68	0.08	0.00	0.00	0.00	0.00
Electric fences	35,010.90	0.70	145.58	0.01	0.00	0.00	0.00	0.00
LED and fluorescent lights (110 V)	57,409.62	1.14	436.75	0.03	0.00	0.00	0.00	0.00
Portable line and others	174,979.46	3.49	727.92	0.05	0.00	0.00	0.00	0.00
Mini ("pico") SHS	157,488.48	3.14	20,090.72	1.38	60.15	0.02	325.90	0.21
Televisions	88,021.09	1.75	6,551.32	0.45	0.00	0.00	0.00	0.00
Generators	386,374.34	7.70	57,942.80	3.98	300.74	0.10	543.17	0.35
Urban SHS	284,076.93	5.66	17,470.19	1.20	115,363.70	38.36	1,691.58	1.09
Solar heaters	33,812.61	0.67	18,343.70	1.26	0.00	0.00	0.00	0.00
Total	**5,015,671.89**	**100**	**1,455,849.18**	**100**	**300,739.57**	**100**	**155,190.77**	**100**

Source: Tecnosol.

competitive market. The inclusion of rural entrepreneurs into the company's distribution channel has provided new jobs and sources of income to its customers, making the firm a more inclusive business. And Tecnosol's value proposition for each of its customer segments has allowed for growth through the specialized products and services the company offers. Each of these innovations helps to advance sustainable energy in Central America.

Although Tecnosol innovates mostly through its business model rather than through technology, the company is nonetheless an example of reverse innovation, Govindarajan and Ramamurti's term for technology or business strategy that is first adopted in the developing world before spreading to industrialized countries.[6] Distributing capital at low costs, powered by microfinance, is a replicable practice not only for the rest of the developing world but also for impoverished zones in the developed world.

Tecnosol's commitment to sustainability may be further understood by drawing on Forest Reinhardt and Richard Vietor's matrix of environmental strategies.[7] This matrix analyzes the purpose of a company's sustainability strategy, from simple compliance to competitive advantage to sustainability. It also analyzes the focus of a company's strategy, from changing its own behavior, to changing the entire market's behavior through competition or regulation. The very nature of Tecnosol's business—renewable energy—speaks to the company's sustainability purpose: seeking competitive advantage and environmental sustainability. The company's strategic focus is still on changing the firm's behavior, but increasing awareness about renewables and the firm's own success contribute to changes at the market level. The increased competition Tecnosol has faced in recent years is evidence of wider change.

Tecnosol's business model provides tangible private and social benefits at the triple bottom line (as defined by John Elkington in 1994[8]), strengthening its claim as a sustainable business. Put simply, the firm is profitable, it dramatically improves the quality of life for thousands of people by creating access to electricity and enabling them to engage in productive activities, and it is environmentally friendly.

Tecnosol's inclusive business model moves beyond traditional notions of corporate social responsibility (CSR). The company is not only in the business of renewable energy but also of empowering rural, low-income Nicaraguans by providing affordable energy solutions. We describe this impact in detail in the following section.

Tecnosol's Impact

A series of best practices have made it possible for Tecnosol to bring electricity to over half a million people. By offering innovative micro-credit financing, the company has challenged the limits of purchasing power. Tecnosol has supplied high-quality products that meet multiple rural needs, boost economic productivity, improve health and education, and enhance entertainment options. Finally, the company delivers at the triple bottom line, bringing social, economic, and environmental benefits to the communities it serves.

Tecnosol has helped improve quality of life in a variety of other ways, too. Customers with SHSs are no longer exposed to indoor air polluted by wood fires or kerosene. Between 1998, when the company was founded, and 2015, more than 300,000 kerosene lamps were removed from circulation as a direct result of its installations. Clients are also less exposed to accidents or fires caused by using candles for lighting, a common practice in rural areas without electricity. With electricity, communities have also gained greater access to communication networks like radio and television. Solar-powered clinics have made it possible to provide medical services at night, enabling clinics to better tend to emergencies. Better lighting has made surgery safer, and solar refrigerators have helped to preserve vaccines and foods, critical to disease prevention. Electric water pumps have enabled access to clean water for all purposes, including medical and residential consumption. At an educational level, electricity has provided students with longer, safer hours of study.

Tecnosol's clients have also benefited economically because they no longer need to purchase kerosene, leading to the annual savings of about US$340 we mentioned above.[9] These savings typically allow clients to repay their SHS investment within three years. In all, Tecnosol reports that its clientele saves up to US$11.5 million that would otherwise have been spent each year on kerosene or batteries. In addition, small convenience store and local retailer revenues have increased, as solar power has made longer business hours possible and solar refrigerators have allowed storage of perishable goods. Local entrepreneurs have also benefited, as they were able to become local solar distributors and earn additional income from their sales.

Finally, aside from the economic and social benefits described above, Tecnosol's solar solutions have generated important environmental benefits. By replacing more than 300,000 kerosene lamps, Tecnosol solar systems reduce carbon dioxide emissions by 9,500 tons each year.[10] The company has also sought to replace existing lead batteries with more efficient lithium batteries. Though lithium batteries cost more, they are more efficient and have a longer lifespan. Although the company buys old batteries back from clients, and offers a discount on new battery purchases, not all batteries get collected. This waste stream makes the prompt switch to lithium batteries even more desirable.

Tecnosol has received a number of awards for its social, economic, and environmental work, among them the Renewable Energy and Energy Saving Award (ERA) in Nicaragua in 2010, first place in the Ashden Awards for Sustainable Energy in England in 2010, the IDB's Excellency in Development in 2010, and the Nicaraguan Chamber of Commerce Excellence in Services Award in 2011. Since 2011, Tecnosol has been ISO 9001:2008 certified. In 2015, Delagneau was selected as one of the social entrepreneurs of his generation by I3 LATAM, an initiative that acknowledges the best social entrepreneurs in the region and brings them together at an entrepreneurship forum. The company has also been recognized internationally by the IDB and the Schwab Foundation for Social Entrepreneurship.

Conclusion

Vladimir Delagneau knew that his business model operated with small gross margins and was therefore heavily dependent on market expansion. His initial expansion strategy faced a series of limitations in terms of capital needs. Although Tecnosol sells in high volume to rural areas, the company's prices have had to remain low because of the limited purchasing power of rural clients. Due to Tecnosol's CSR commitment and its low-income target market, Delagneau believes it is important to further reduce costs so more people can gain access to electricity and its benefits. Perhaps increasing prices for urban customers (where most clients have medium to high incomes) could alleviate some of the pressure on the rural sales that Delagneau has committed to continuing. In addition, improved technology is likely to bring even more competition to the urban sector, and Tecnosol will have to revise its value proposition for new urban consumers. Tecnosol's sustainability strategy must also become more explicit, especially its reporting mechanisms. Up until now, the firm's reporting has been mostly informal. The company has highlighted energy savings at conferences but not on the Tecnosol website. Tecnosol hopes to improve on all of these fronts. To that end, Delagneau has enrolled in an executive MBA program at a prestigious Latin American business school.

In the meantime, a few key drivers have continued to push the firm forward. The company has been propelled by Delagneau's leadership and commitment to increasing clean energy access. In addition, the firm has built a strong reputation based on performance, and has expanded its network of clients, large and small. An unmet demand for electricity in energy-poor Central America continues to drive growth and make NGOs, international financial institutions, and governments natural allies. Solar technology's increased affordability and efficiency have boosted profits, especially as the firm has sought to increase its presence in the urban market. And, finally, microfinance institutions and rural banks have made it possible to sell energy systems in cash-strapped rural communities. Multilateral institutions are also drivers of this sort, reducing risks for Tecnosol and enabling higher sales volumes.

Tecnosol's success in Central America has policy implications for governments struggling with low electrification rates and the cost of keeping up with energy technology. Public-private partnerships with firms like Tecnosol can create business opportunities for private firms and also deliver public services governments might not otherwise be able to provide. Robust business sustainability strategies can be replicated anywhere in the developing world and create worthwhile and durable investments.

Chapter 6

RIZEK PUSHES THE DOMINICAN REPUBLIC COCOA INDUSTRY TOWARD SUSTAINABILITY

Milagros De Camps Germán

Abstract

Rizek Cacao, the leading cocoa exporter in the Dominican Republic, faced complete collapse after Hurricane Georges devastated the island nation in 1998. Since cocoa beans grow best under forest cover, the threat to the industry also posed a threat to Dominican forests. However, the company regrouped, changed its strategies and, in the process, helped resurrect the industry in the Dominican Republic, which now ranks among the world's top ten cocoa bean producers. The disaster prompted Rizek Cacao to develop a best practice for the industry, the formation in 2001 of FUPAROCA, the Foundation for Social Assistance, Recovery, and Management of Organic Cocoa Plantations. As a non-profit organization, FUPAROCA operates under the umbrella of Rizek Cacao but is run independently from the company. The flagship social responsibility initiative of Rizek Cacao, FUPAROCA is managed by 4,000 independent cocoa growers. The organization promotes capacity building, education, and technical support to improve production of cocoa certified as organic, advocate sustainable farming practices, and provide the highest quality production standards in the industry. These practices have expanded organic cocoa production, supported environment and forest protection, and bolstered the quality of life of cocoa growers and their families. FUPAROCA has also transformed Rizek's public image, increased its revenues, and improved consumer brand loyalty.

Introduction

Hurricane Georges swept through the Dominican Republic in September 1998, devastating the country's cocoa production. Almost two-thirds of cocoa crops were destroyed by the storm and its aftereffects. Rather than fold and walk away, Rizek Cacao, the leading cocoa exporter in the country, saw opportunity amid the crisis. Out of the devastation rose a new strategic awareness for the company, summed up by Hector Rizek, president of Rizek Cacao, who asked his management team, "What will we do? Where are we headed? How do we protect ourselves from a future economic turndown?"

Rizek Cacao's Best Practice

In 2001, Hector Rizek's team responded by forming the Foundation for Social Assistance, Recovery, Management of Organic Cocoa Plantations, known by its Spanish acronym FUPAROCA. Organized as a non-profit, FUPAROCA operates under the umbrella of Rizek Cacao but is managed independently from the company. Although it does represent the primary corporate social responsibility (CSR) initiative of Rizek Cacao, FUPAROCA is managed by 4,000 independent cocoa farmers whose purpose is to promote capacity building, education, and technical support for certified cocoa production, sustainable farming practices, and the highest quality production standards in the industry. The practices of these 4,000 growers contribute to the protection of the environment, bio-diversity, and quality of life of cocoa growers and their families.

The Dominican Cocoa Industry

Theobroma cacao is the bean used to manufacture chocolate, deriving its name from the Greek word for "food of the Gods." These cocoa beans can only be grown and produced in countries located in the belt between ten degrees latitude north and south of the Equator. Beans grow best under forest cover, which is why approximately 375,600 acres of forest in the Dominican Republic are currently used by cocoa plantations.

The Dominican Republic is the ninth-largest exporter of cocoa beans in the world, sending its products to the United States and Europe, with a growing presence in Asia. The country has a favorable climate for cocoa production. These favorable growing conditions, coupled with the genetic resistance of Dominican trees to cocoa-damaging plagues, has propelled the Dominican Republic to become the world's leading exporter of certified organic and fair trade cocoa. The nation has a 40 percent share of the world market for certified organic and fair trade cocoa. Cocoa production provides economic benefit to the Dominican Republic, and also protection of rainforest ecosystems and growing international recognition for the country.

Historically, cocoa beans from the Dominican Republic had a bad reputation in international markets due to their poor quality. Sustainably produced cocoa represented only 20 percent of the market share in the mid-1980s. Production in the country reached its all-time low in the years 1998 and 1999, as hurricane damage followed the lowest cocoa prices since the mid-1960s. In 1999, the price for a metric ton of cocoa beans was US$861, a steep drop from the all-time high of US$4,361.58 per metric ton in 1977. This dire situation nearly destroyed the Dominican cocoa industry completely. In the wake of Hurricane Georges, cocoa production decreased from 70,000 metric tons in the 1997–98 growing season to 25,000 metric tons in 1998–99,[1] and cocoa export earnings fell by 75 percent. This was a major loss for the US$214 million industry.[2]

In order to understand how Rizek Cacao came to bolster the Dominican organic cocoa industry through FUPAROCA, we first need to understand who the industry's actors are. The industry in the Dominican Republic is comprised of approximately 40,000 smallholder growers and some medium and large landowners. Extensive commercial plantations are less common due partly to the size of the country, which occupies the eastern two-thirds of the island of Hispaniola and covers only 18,705 square miles.

The typical profile of a Dominican cocoa grower is a male in his late fifties who lives modestly and owns a small plot of land (2.5 hectares, on average) where he produces cocoa and other agricultural products for the export market. The seasonality of the industry is often at odds with demands of a low-income family like rent, school expenses, transport, health, communication, and utilities. Seasonality also makes organized financial planning a challenge.[3] Because financing from lending institutions to increase productivity is unavailable to these smallholder growers, their "crop yields are low, profitability is negligible, and farmer incomes subsequently remain at poverty level."[4]

In the cocoa industry, growers traditionally bear all the risks of the production process, as they are responsible for the cultivation, harvest, threshing, fermentation, and drying of the crop. The individual growers then deliver the product to an intermediary or a broker who distributes it to exporters. Rizek Cacao transformed this traditional business model by identifying new economic opportunities, diversifying its business, and taking a chance on a new more sustainable approach to cocoa production. In so doing, the company created new revenue streams for the company, protected forests by securing the continued viability of cocoa crops, improved the livelihoods of smallholder growers, expanded the area of production certified organic, and generated value for the whole supply chain.

Rizek's History

"Don" Nazario Rizek, a Palestinian immigrant, arrived in the Dominican Republic in the late nineteenth century. In 1905, he founded a small family company that commercialized agricultural products, including cocoa. Over the years, Rizek expanded his business and concentrated investments on large-scale agricultural land acquisition. He became the first producer and exporter of cocoa at a time when the industry had been monopolized by the longtime dictatorship of Generalissimo Rafael Trujillo, who was assassinated in 1961. By 1965, the company was the largest producer of cocoa in the country.

Today, Rizek Cacao is the largest cocoa exporter in the Dominican Republic by volume (see Figure 6.1). The company produces, processes, and commercializes cocoa beans as well as their derivatives for use in the global chocolate industry. It meets high-quality standards and, as

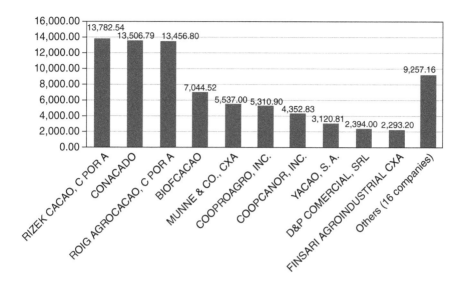

Figure 6.1 Cocoa exports, Dominican Republic, 2014/2015 (metric tons).
Source: Dominican Republic Ministry of Agriculture, email to author May 19, 2016.

a result, its product is targeted at the luxury food market. Of the 25 Dominican companies that participate in the cocoa market, Rizek has the biggest share, controlling 17.2 percent of the market. The company has been locally and internationally recognized as a leader in promoting sustainable business practices, notably by its CSR program, protection of the environment, and promotion of national economic growth.

Rizek's production comes from 43 privately owned farms and a network of 8,000 small cocoa growers. The company operates a modern system of quality control that traces its cocoa crops throughout all the steps of the supply chain, including the identification and codification of trees and the logistics of the industrial process. Leading up to the devastating damage to crops caused by Hurricane Georges, Rizek's business structure was dependent largely on the small landowners who supplied it with most of its crop. This inevitably undermined the integrity of the company's business model, as it relied on lending to small producers to sustain its operation. These loans created enormous debts for small producers who were often unable to meet their financial obligations. Following the hurricane, in order to avoid a massive rural exodus or transition to short-cycle alternatives to cocoa crops, a group of exporters led by Rizek joined forces to bail out smallholder growers. The Agricultural Bank, along with the Reserves Bank (both state-owned financial institutions), financed exporters who subsequently lent to smallholder growers to keep the cocoa sector active in what was called the "Contribución Solidaria." The exporters became collection agents for the banks and paid the debt in full by 2008. This joint bailout offered a boost to the cocoa industry during a time of crisis.

After the hurricane, the company recognized the cocoa industry's economic system was unreliable. In 2006, Rizek modified its business model to centralize the production process in order to create shared value to all industry actors, including smallholder growers. At the time, consumers in developed markets were becoming more conscious of the social, environmental, and health benefits of sustainably produced products. The demand for organic cocoa was rapidly rising while supply remained stagnant. With the financing available to invest in this more environmentally friendly crop, the market for a differentiated product arose—certified organic, fine-aroma cocoa, protected designation of origin, or other kinds of specialty cocoa that could differentiate the Dominican crop from other beans.

FUPAROCA had been founded in 2001. As Rizek adjusted its business strategy to reduce vulnerability to disasters and invest in a differentiated product, however, the FUPAROCA became an integral part of Rizek's business model.

FUPAROCA now exists under the umbrella of Rizek Cacao and is focused on rehabilitating and certifying cocoa plantations for a variety of international standards. Through the organization, the company also provides technical support and capacity building to producers in order to achieve optimal production and to meet international certification standards like Rainforest Alliance, Organic, UTZ, Kosher, Bio Swiss, Japanese Agricultural Standards, and European Standards. Each certification process is demanding and requires an international control system that traces the product through all steps of the supply chain. FUPAROCA also educates farmers on production management, grafting, environmental protection, health and hygiene, child labor, gender issues, waste disposal, chemical use, and water treatment.

Sustainability Analysis

On top of the challenges posed by Hurricane Georges, Rizek realized that the Dominican Republic was in a difficult position because the country could not compete with the scale of production in West African countries. Instead, it concentrated on producing high-quality cocoa for the luxury food market. In this way, Rizek was able to differentiate itself from international competitors. Rizek has led the transformation of the Dominican cocoa industry by appealing to the high-end market through product certifications. Now, the industry is almost entirely certified, and able to take advantage of the environmental benefits those certifications provide.

Furthermore, Rizek is currently the only company in the Dominican cocoa industry investing in research and development. As a result, it has identified species that provide better-quality seeds and rootstocks through its DNA sequencing program. These seedlings and rootstocks are currently being used for production by Rizek partners and provide better yield and stronger resistance to diseases.

Rizek's new approach has addressed the disparity between the growing international market and the weakening local system of production. The company has taken a defensive certification approach to bad industry actors and a proactive certification approach toward European and US consumers willing to pay a premium for differentiated products. At first, the process was not smooth. A learning curve came with this approach, presenting additional challenges to the certification efforts.

FUPAROCA is also a vehicle for Rizek to invest responsibly while generating community benefit. Through FUPAROCA, Rizek provides education to farmers on sustainable agriculture, emphasizing technical matters like shade management and the prevention of forest fires. It also promotes conservation and responsible labor practices (such as freedom of movement, avoiding child labor, preventing discrimination, living wages, occupational safety, and health conditions). Rizek and

FUPAROCA provide access to farming inputs to improve the quality of the final cocoa product. Finally, the company has initiated several community support activities, such as building schools, bridges, and infrastructure for running water. These investments also extend to the improvement of cocoa crops.

Importantly, preserving the Dominican cocoa industry also means preserving the country's forests. In Hector Rizek's words, "We can't overestimate the significance of sustainability to the cocoa sector." The crop is planted in Dominican Republic's primary forests. Today, 40 percent of the Dominican Republic's forest is dedicated to cocoa and around 40 percent of the country's rivers originate in the forested highlands. "Cocoa is one of our national treasures, and so we have to protect it," Rizek said.

Rizek's certification-based sustainability approach did not come without risk. Notably, Rizek invested resources and capacity in product certifications on the premise that the signal of sustainability leadership would differentiate its business from the competition. But this strategy was far from a sure thing. If Rizek's investments in sustainability hadn't resulted in enhanced market status, it would have had sunk costs to bear with no pathway to recover the expense.

Challenges

Currently, although consumers are demanding more certified products and chocolate companies are becoming stricter about the sources of their beans, the business model centered on a differentiated product—certified cocoa—is starting to lose its appeal. In the past decade, the cocoa industry has registered a decrease in the value of certified cocoa on the international market. Rizek understands that its competitiveness based on certifications is decreasing and that certification is not enough for differentiation and value creation in the cocoa industry.

Furthermore, the low productivity of aging cocoa plants, lack of access to finance for small growers, and the volatility in cocoa prices will always remain a challenge for the cocoa industry. Finally, more than 90 percent of the cocoa in the Dominican Republic is sold internationally. A portion of the remaining cocoa is processed in the country for local consumption in the form of chocolate bars for hot cocoa while the rest is later exported in the form of cocoa butter and other cocoa-based products.[5] This form of value-added cocoa production for more developed countries is one of the most profitable businesses in the world, and despite attempts, Rizek has not been able to break into this market.

Because of these challenges, the company's vision for the near future is to develop an innovative business model centered around agricultural real estate. Under this model, Rizek will sell plots of land planted with better-quality crops of cocoa and companion crops beneficial to cocoa, guaranteeing growers the purchase of all their production and creating an alternative revenue stream. This new model will provide an attractive mode of entry for new producers and for farmers wishing to expand their production.

Conclusion

Rizek has improved the public image of the company and the country while also retaining employee and consumer loyalty. By working to certify its production, the company has not only preserved an industry that helps to protect forests and expanded the presence of organic cocoa production in the Dominican Republic. It has also achieved its goal of creating a differentiated product and gained a competitive edge over other participants in the market. This increased competitiveness has resulted in a significant increase in revenue and improved return on investment and operating earnings. The demand for specific cocoa flavors has created a niche market for the organization and it has been recognized by consumers for its high-quality products. This recognition has guaranteed loyalty not only from consumers, but from all the actors that participate in the company's supply chain.

Consequently, Rizek Cacao has strengthened its brand. It has begun to charge a premium over its previous product prices; increased operational efficiency; minimized risks; reduced costs by negotiating better agreements with suppliers; and created stronger relationships with big-name manufacturing brands such as Mars, Nestle, and Valrhona. Rizek has identified new business opportunities, which give the company greater flexibility in responding to future economic downturns and better opportunities for cocoa growers and employees of the company.

Rizek has helped to drive the transformation of the cocoa industry in the Dominican Republic and position the country as an exporter of high-quality beans. In the wake of Hurricane Georges, such a transformation may have seemed impossible.

Chapter 7

CENTROSUR LEADS THE WAY TO SUSTAINABILITY IN ECUADOR

Edwin Garcia

Abstract

Utility companies in Ecuador are required to compile annual reports summarizing the environmental impacts of their operations. However, the Empresa Eléctrica Centro Sur C.A. (CENTROSUR), a government-owned electricity distributor, has taken this requirement a step further by being the first utility company in Ecuador to implement practices designed to *reduce* overall impact on the environment. By doing so, CENTROSUR demonstrates that sustainability is not just the company's responsibility, but also a business opportunity that could be embraced by other enterprises. This case study shows how CENTROSUR has been able to reduce its environmental impact through the implementation of an innovative recycling program called *Sistema Integral de Manejo de Materiales, Equipos y Desechos Generados*, better known by its acronym SIMED. Furthermore, this recycling program provides CENTROSUR with indicators that can be used to track the quantity of materials being reused, sold for scrap, or properly discarded. Each of these metrics has helped the company boost its bottom line. The SIMED program demonstrates the economic value of going beyond minimum regulatory requirements on environmental issues by generating over US$2 million in revenue for CENTROSUR.

In collaboration with Juan Vasquez (engineer and Environment Department director, Empresa Electrica Regional Centro sur C.A.).

Introduction

CENTROSUR, a government-owned electric utility in southern Ecuador, has found ways to reduce the waste it generates on its projects. The company was founded in 1950 as the Empresa Eléctrica Miraflores S.A., a government-owned and -operated company (later renamed Empresa Eléctrica Centro Sur C.A. or CENTROSUR). It created and generated electricity until 1999, when Ecuador's Ministry of Energy mandated that the company focus solely on distribution. Today, the company is headquartered in Cuenca, the capital city of Azuay province, in southern Ecuador. CENTROSUR now supplies energy to Azuay, Morona-Santiago, and Cañar provinces, an area covering 23,759 square miles with a population of more than one million people according to the most recent census in 2010. With a yearly installation capacity of 1,018 gigawatt hours (GWh), the company serves 368,648 customers. Of these customers, 88 percent are households, 9 percent are commercial enterprises, and 2 percent are industrial users. As of 2015, the company had 476 full-time employees, 116 part-time staff, and annual revenues of US$106 million. All the electricity the company distributes is generated by hydroelectric power.

The Best Practice

As part of its corporate social responsibility (CSR) strategy, CENTROSUR has implemented a multifaceted program called *Sistema Integral de Manejo de Materiales, Equipos y Desechos Generados* (SIMED), translated as "system for the handling of materials, equipment and waste." The initiative has measurably reduced the company's energy consumption, waste, and impact on the environment. As a regional utility, energy efficiency at CENTROSUR reduces pressure on the electrical grid.

Sustainability Strategy

SIMED is part of a wider effort by CENTROSUR to be mindful of behaviors within the company that impact the environment and change those behaviors if that impact is negative. However, the company's sustainability strategy also includes outreach to customers to encourage them to change their own behavior. It is through these initiatives that the company aims to reduce its carbon footprint and reward customers for their energy-saving efforts. This section discusses each arm of CENTROSUR's wider sustainability strategy.

Plan Renova *(Plan Renew)*

The main objective of *Plan Renova* is to encourage customers to replace refrigerators that are 10 years old or older with new refrigerators that are up to four times more energy-efficient. Through this program, any residential customer who is up-to-date on bill payments with a monthly energy use not exceeding 200 kilowatt hours (kWh) qualifies for the removal of their old refrigerator and a US$200 rebate toward the purchase of a new one. Since the inception of the program in 2012, a total of 5,000 energy-inefficient refrigerators have been replaced.

Light Bulb Recycling Program

Between 2009 and 2012, CENTROSUR ran a campaign to encourage residential customers to switch from incandescent light bulbs to energy-efficient ones, during which time approximately 800,000 inefficient bulbs were replaced.[1] The company solved one problem but created another one: the energy-efficient light bulbs contained mercury, barium, and strontium. Although not harmful in small amounts, the total quantity of these elements, based on the number of bulbs now in use, could cause health hazards if the bulbs are not disposed of properly. Awareness of this hazard spurred the company to recover the energy-efficient light bulbs no longer in use and follow proper environmental protocol for their disposal. To get its message out, CENTROSUR used a local newspaper to communicate with its customers. The company also invested US$14,000 in a machine that would disassemble the bulbs and remove the mercury safely. The device allowed CENTROSUR to dispose of the bulbs without causing harm to the environment. Through the light bulb recycling program, the company reported that it had properly disposed of a total of 27,038 units in 2015.[2]

Luz de Nuestro Sol *(Light from Our Sun)*

The *Luz de Nuestro Sol* program provides electricity to rural areas of Ecuador's Amazon region by supplying and installing photovoltaic (PV) solar panels. The PV panels are delivered to individual communities and company professionals train each community's leader to install, maintain, and troubleshoot the technology. To date, approximately 3,264 families in the Amazon region have benefited from this program through access to electric appliances, TVs, computers, and light in the evenings.[3] Because of *Luz de Nuestro Sol*, children in these communities can now study and do homework without relying on candles. Without PV panels, families would spend US$22.73 per month on candles, batteries, and fuel for electrical generators,[4] but the new technology costs just US$2.40 per month, saving families a monthly average of US$20.33.

Yo Cuido mi Energia *(I Am Conscious of My Energy Use)*

An awareness-raising campaign targeting residential and industrial customers, *Yo Cuido mi Energia* encourages people to reduce their energy use by offering helpful information. CENTROSUR provides guidance on choosing energy-efficient appliances, turning lights off when not in use, running washers and dryers at off-peak hours, and more. The campaign is communicated via the company's web page, social media, radio stations, and customers' monthly bills. The program also helps consumers become more knowledgeable about their energy use and provides estimates of cost savings. To date, there is no information available to measure the effectiveness of this program.

Induction Cooking and Water Heated by Electricity

For years, Ecuadorians have used natural gas for cooking and hot water needs, made possible by annual government gas subsidies of US$700 million. However, Ecuador has the potential to supply electricity to customers without natural gas or subsidies. For this reason, eight hydroelectric projects started generating electricity in 2016, two of which are directly connected to the company.[5] As an incentive for customers to switch from natural gas–powered stoves, CENTROSUR is offering rebates toward the purchase of electric stoves. Ultimately, the government will save money too, as people become less dependent on natural gas subsidies.

Sustainability Analysis

This analysis focuses on the SIMED arm of CENTROSUR's sustainability strategy. In early 2007, the consulting firm Efficacitas brought to CENTROSUR's attention the existence of materials, equipment, oils, and waste left at abandoned job sites and warehouses (see Figures 7.1–7.3). At the same time, a new electrical substation under construction was in danger of being stopped by residents of the Amazon region for its negative environmental impact. As a result of this conflict, Francisco Carrasco Astudillo, the company's president, hired engineer Juan Vasquez to oversee the company's Environmental Department and help gain the trust of Amazonian residents. With greater community buy-in, the substation project could continue while the company found solutions to its environmental problems. An expert on clean energy production, Vasquez immediately started to work on a solution to the excessive materials being left on job sites. Inspired by a documentary he saw on the National Geographic television network about recycling, he began an in-house waste-reduction program that became SIMED. The program was created to reduce, reuse, recycle, or safely discard all excess materials, equipment, and waste from the projects CENTROSUR hires out to independent contractors.

SIMED now covers all materials used on projects. These materials—such as concrete, wood posts, glass, ceramic insulators, and large power transformers—are now being reused, sold for parts, or sent to landfills. The large power transformers being taken out of service were of particular concern since they contain hazardous oils. The SIMED program relies on contractors to haul all residuals to the company's warehouse where an inventory can be taken and the material properly handled and, if necessary, discarded (see Figures 7.4 and 7.5).

Figure 7.1 Materials left on job sites.
Source: Juan Vasquez, CENTROSUR.

Figure 7.2 Materials left on job sites.
Source: Juan Vasquez, CENTROSUR.

Figure 7.3 Materials left on job sites.
Source: Juan Vasquez, CENTROSUR.

Figure 7.4 Contractors bringing materials back to the company's warehouse in Cuenca.
Source: Juan Vasquez, CENTROSUR.

Figure 7.5 Contractors bringing materials back to the company's warehouse in Cuenca.
Source: Juan Vasquez, CENTROSUR.

A best practice for CENTROSUR is the SIMED requirement that contractors bring excess materials back to the CENTROSUR ware-house. If they fail to do this, they forfeit any future work with the company.

Once contractors return the material, CENTROSUR can separate hazardous materials from nonhazardous ones (see Figures 7.6 through 7.10). Hazardous materials include items like toners, fibers, and

Figure 7.6 Materials being dismantled and separated for resale.
Source: Juan Vasquez, CENTROSUR.

Figure 7.7 Materials being dismantled and separated for resale.
Source: Juan Vasquez, CENTROSUR.

fluorescent lamps, which are sealed in 55-gallon tanks for temporary storage and delivered to ETAPA-EMAC, the sanitation department of Cuenca, for proper disposal.[6] Hazardous materials that are not currently treatable are safely stored until new regulations or solutions can be implemented. For better tracking, the company's IT Department developed software that records how much material is recovered, sold, and sent to landfills. These indicators have allowed engineers to quantify economic returns, which is key to keeping the SIMED program alive and maintaining support from the front office of CENTROSUR.

Nonhazardous materials brought back from work sites are further subdivided into three categories[7]:

Figure 7.8 Materials being dismantled and separated for resale.
Source: Juan Vasquez, CENTROSUR.

Figure 7.9 Materials being dismantled and separated for resale.
Source: Juan Vasquez, CENTROSUR.

Figure 7.10 Materials being dismantled and separated for resale.
Source: Juan Vasquez, CENTROSUR.

- *Reusable materials* such as ceramic insulators are entered into the inventory program for their future reuse on new projects.
- *Waste that does not require processing* is subdivided into recyclables and landfill material. Recyclables are sold to third parties.
- *Materials in need of further treatment* are dismantled and sold to certified buyers in compliance with environmental regulations.

SIMED provides clear environmental advantages to CENTROSUR. Since SIMED began operations, approximately 1,500 tons of materials have been recovered, recycled, reused, or properly disposed of. Software has allowed the program, as seen in the tables below, to identify inputs and outputs and quantify economic benefits to the company. CENTROSUR currently benefits from SIMED through the new revenue streams it creates as well. The program is cost effective because it allows the reuse of materials for new projects, and the sale of recyclable materials like metal.

Table 7.1 shows the total number of toners recovered, encapsulated, and sent to ETAPA-EMAC for proper disposal. A high quantity of toners were disposed of between 2008 and 2010, because they had accumulated for years and the company had many projects in operation. After 2011, the number of projects decreased, and as a result less material was needed. Table 7.2 shows the number of light bulbs recovered between 2008 and 2015. After the chemicals were extracted, they were packaged and delivered to ETAPA-EMAC for disposal. Quantities fluctuate because of the variability in customer return rate, since the program relies heavily on customers bringing the light bulbs back. Table 7.3 shows the total hazardous materials collected from the SIMED program. The company sent these materials to ETAPA-EMAC for disposal. These values also fluctuate based on the number of projects. In 2011, for instance, the company dedicated a large part of its budget to distribution lines, and as a result installed new transformers. Table 7.4 shows materials collected from projects and sent to landfills when a buyer could not be found. Differences in quantities reflect the number of projects the company completes per year. Plastic and glass are the most frequently collected materials. Table 7.5 shows the total quantities of metals recovered between 2009 and 2015,

Table 7.1 Total toners recovered and encapsulated

Description	Quantity	Year
	758	2008
	755	2009
	1,002	2010
Various toners	614	2011
	275	2012
	164	2013
	11	2014
Total recovered as of 2014	**3,579**	

Source: CENTROSUR.

Table 7.2 Total light bulbs recovered from recycling program

Description	Quantity	Year
	7,265	2008
	12,436	2009
Lamps with sodium and magnesium	8,023	2010
vapor, fluorescent and others	12,205	2011
	10,548	2012
	12,393	2013
	13,228	2014
	17,619	2015
Total recovered as of 2015	**93,717**	

Source: CENTROSUR.

with aluminum being the most recycled metal. Once metals such as aluminum have been properly separated, they are sold to local buyers. For example, Indalum, a cookware manufacturer in Cuenca, buys almost all of the recyclable aluminum for its manufacturing processes. At the end of 2015, SIMED staff reported that it had generated more than US$2.4 million of extra income for CENTROSUR.

Challenges

Many challenges exist in the implementation of SIMED, including insufficient internal company support, price fluctuations for metals,

Table 7.3 Hazardous materials collected and sent to ETAPA-EMAC

Residues	Units	2009	2010	2011	2012	2013	2014	2015	Total toners recovered
Dielectric oil without PCB	Gallons	1,050	1,410	7,927	3,170	3,505	12,690	3,920	**33,672**
Lubricant oil	Gallons	–	–	–	–	825	–	–	**825**
Nickel–cadmium battery	Units	–	–	35	58	60	29	–	**182**
Lead–acid battery	Units	–	–	259	72	112	272	–	**715**
Diesel	Gallons	–	–	–	–	275	–	–	**275**
Batteries	Kg	–	–	–	11	5	3	–	**19**

Source: CENTROSUR.

Table 7.4 Nonhazardous materials collected and sent to landfills

Waste	Units	2008	2009	2010	2011	2012	2013	2014	2015
Plastic	Pounds	7,489	10,244	9,002	11,492	11,586	13,163	25,626	51,004
Glass	Pounds	4,579	6,349	4,721	5,007	6,123	6,417	12,040	12,932
Wood	Pounds	218	6,319	2,124	1,030	788	1,843	333	17,898
Fabric	Pounds	–	–	–	13.61	2.27	–	479.99	4,230
Rubber	Pounds	–	–	–	3,483	2,799	4,207	3,875	4,107
Total		12,286	22,913	15,848	21,027	21,299	25,633	42,356	90,173

Source: CENTROSUR.

Table 7.5 Total metal recovered

Year	Weight (pounds)	Material	%
2009	1,083,253	Aluminum	51.29
2010	484,692	Iron	14.32
2011	344,366	Steel	5.73
2012	489,207	Copper	2.34
2013	545,126	Others	26.32
2015	579,056.38		

Source: CENTROSUR.

and a limited market for nonmetal materials. The lack of continuous support from within CENTROSUR is the greatest of these challenges, and stems in part from the absence of social and regulatory demand for sustainable practices. If the national government in Quito prioritizes sustainability, this could change.

Sustainability is still seen by some CENTROSUR departments as a burden for a company whose only purpose, they insist, is to achieve regulatory compliance. Furthermore, because of these ingrained perspectives, there is no formal budget assigned to the Environmental Department and it has grown little since SIMED was first implemented.

The nonexistent market for recovered nonmetal materials also limits SIMED, forcing the company to send these nonmetals to landfills. Once an alternative to the disposal of some of these materials is found, the company's revenue will further increase. For this reason, CENTROSUR has said it will sign an agreement with a third party to find a viable reuse of these materials. Additionally, the company is seeking a manufacturer who might be able to buy glass for other industrial processes.

Finally, it has been difficult to gain customer recognition of the progress CENTROSUR is making to reduce its environmental footprint. Customer surveys exist but seldom ask about CENTROSUR's sustainability practices.

Recommendations

There are numerous areas for CENTROSUR to potentially improve its environmental practices. For example, better management of electrification projects could help further reduce the unnecessary use of materials, equipment, and tools. Better project management could provide superior ways to make use of materials, more efficient construction methods, and more precise estimates of materials needed for each project, thus reducing excess. Also, the company should ask these questions when it starts a new project:

1. Why are we using each type of material?
2. Are there any more sustainable substitutes?
3. What areas of projects generate the most waste?

These questions will help CENTROSUR reduce its use of materials at the beginning of each project and decrease the amount of waste that needs to be managed at the end. Collaboration with suppliers on improving project design would aid in even greater reduction of material use.

CENTROSUR also needs more detailed information on the cost of implementing sustainability programs like SIMED to determine their profitability. At the moment, CENTROSUR does not have information on the amount it has invested in its sustainability initiatives or whether or not they are being accounted for when calculating new profits. For instance, SIMED makes use of the company's existing infrastructure to store and process the materials brought back by contractors, but this is not accounted for in the results. The company, for example, now pays to send nonhazardous materials to landfills. CENTROSUR should formally account for this when considering the impact of SIMED.

Conclusion

As CENTROSUR looks to the future, the company's Environmental Department believes that prioritizing sustainability does more than just offer a way to comply with regulation. In fact, a good sustainability program can provide a company with a new way to generate income while reducing its environmental footprint. The more than US$2 million in revenue CENTROSUR has gained from the sale of recycled metals demonstrates these benefits, not to mention the positive social and environmental impacts of properly disposing of 1,500 tons of other materials. However, the lack of support from within the company has meant that each year a new plan for improving the SIMED program falls short of full implementation. Since its initial creation, SIMED has undergone few changes to match its quickly changing economic environment, and the program is no longer the integral part of company operations that it should be. In fact, the program garnered just a passing mention in CENTROSUR's most recent annual CSR report.

Regardless of these shortcomings, CENTROSUR still serves as an example for other companies looking to implement similar environmental programs. SIMED offers an example of how to stop seeing a company's waste as a burden and, instead, see it as an opportunity to reduce, reuse, and recycle while simultaneously increasing profitability.

Chapter 8

A RESILIENT WORLD: BAVARIA BUILDS ITS CASE ON WATER

Santiago Cortés Villota

Abstract

Bavaria S.A.'s partnership with SABMiller in 2005 was a sound strategic move for the two beer companies from both business and sustainability perspectives. The resultant company, Bavaria SABMiller, was then able to partner with the World Wildlife Fund (WWF) to improve its water use and management. In late 2016, Anheuser-Busch InBev acquired SABMiller. Bavaria—headquartered in Bogotá, Colombia—has developed a consolidated sustainability strategy around five "world" visions that represent the company's commitment to the environment: Thriving World, Sociable World, Resilient World, Clean World, and Productive World. This case study focuses on the Resilient World program, outlining the relationship between Bavaria and water—the fundamental resource for beer production and, hence, for the life of the company. The chapter lays out how Bavaria uses real-time monitoring information to regulate its water use. It also analyzes how the company has relied on strategic partnerships, leadership, and organizational culture to go beyond compliance and deploy ambitious sustainability initiatives. It then describes the key challenges Bavaria has faced in implementing this strategy, recognizing that continuous learning will improve sustainability.

Introduction

The foundation of the largest beer company in Colombia dates back to 1889, when two pairs of brothers—Leo and Emil Kopp from Germany, and Santiago and Carlos Arturo Castello from Colombia—joined forces to purchase land for the construction of a brewery. Although the partnership didn't last long, the Kopp brothers continued their mission and, in 1890, started Bavaria Kopp's Deutsche Bierbrauerei and built San Diego, the first operational beer plant in Bogotá. Over the next two decades, Bavaria established itself as a leader in Colombia's beer industry and became a recognizable name on the international market. Among the company's early accomplishments were the opening of a second brewery in the city of Barranquilla, the launching of its Aguila brand in 1913, the establishment of various strategic alliances (e.g., with Continental Brewery of Medellin), the construction of new plants in Duitama and Bogotá, and the acquisition of the Cucuta and Panama breweries.

By the mid-twentieth century, Bavaria was the second-largest brewery in South America. This steady rise to prominence culminated in 2005, when the London-based multinational brewing company SABMiller acquired Bavaria for US$7.8 billion.[1] At the time, it was one of the most significant mergers in the international beer industry. In October 2016, Anheuser-Busch InBev acquired SABMiller (and, thus, Bavaria) in a US$103 billion merger of the world's two biggest beermakers. Today, with 126 years of profitability, eight operating plants, a production capacity of 26 million hectoliters per year, more than 8,000 direct and indirect employees, and countrywide distribution, Bavaria is an iconic brand in Colombia and a major contributor to the nation's economy.

In 2014, Bavaria adopted SABMiller's global sustainability strategy known as PROSPERAR (which means "to prosper" in Spanish) under the premise that businesses attain prosperity and best results when performing in harmony with the environment and society. The company has remained committed to this strategy even after SABMiller's merger with Anheuser-Busch InBev. Based on five areas (or "worlds")—Thriving, Sociable, Resilient, Clean, and Productive—the strategy is the outcome of a thorough, companywide analysis in which it considered the voices of all relevant stakeholders. The implementation of PROSPERAR relies heavily on partnerships with stakeholders to tackle problems and create holistic solutions.

The Best Practice: Short-Cycle Intervals

Of the five "worlds" that comprise Bavaria's sustainability strategy, Resilient World is the focus of this study. Resilient World focuses on efficient water use in the manufacture of beer and soft drinks, and monitoring the percentage of water inputs that come from safe water sources. Bavaria has found that its best practice under the Resilient World umbrella is the establishment of "short-cycle intervals." The on-the-ground execution of these intervals consists of a 15-minute "conversation" between shifts, in which both operators (the one who finishes one shift and the one who begins the next shift) discuss the processes they are accountable for, including water consumption.

These intervals are now an embedded process within the company's operation culture, allowing the company to generate real-time information about its operations. This information is then consolidated and analyzed on a daily basis, enabling the company to have better control over its water consumption and quickly react to any problem or anomaly that may arise. Prior to implementing the short-cycle interval practice, information about water consumption was gathered, stored, and analyzed on a monthly basis. Short-cycle intervals have allowed Bavaria to decrease response time for potential problems by a factor of 30. As sound as the process may be from an operational efficiency perspective, what makes it a best practice within Bavaria is that it has become naturally embedded within the company's organizational culture. The short-cycle intervals are a particularly effective practice emblematic of the broader water sustainability strategies that make up Resilient World.

Bavaria's Sustainability Strategy

Beer is the third most-consumed beverage in the world, after water and tea. Since 1998, world beer production has increased at a compound annual growth rate of 2.6 percent, and has leveled off in the past three years at between 1.96 and 1.97 billion hectoliters (hl) per year.[2] Asia, Europe, and South America (including Central America) combined represent more than three-quarters of the total global production with

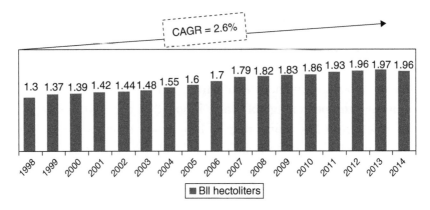

Figure 8.1 Global beer production, 1998–2014.

Source: Statista.com.

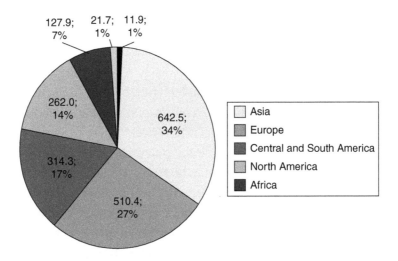

Figure 8.2 Global beer consumption per region, 2014 (in hectoliters).

Source: Kirin Beer University Global Beer Production Report, 2014.

646.7, 515.6, and 328.6 million hl per year, respectively.[3] Consumption figures for these three regions mirror the production numbers—in 2014, the three regions consumed a total of 1.47 billion hl. Figures 8.1 and 8.2 illustrate global production and consumption trends.

Countries in South and Central America have collectively positioned themselves as the third most important region in the global beer industry, with production and consumption that have continuously increased for

Table 8.1 Production and consumption of beer in Colombia

	2013 (millions of hl)	2014 (millions of hl)	Growth rate (2013–14; in %)	Global share (2014; in %)	Global rank (2014)
Production	20.80	20.20	−2.9	1.1	19
Consumption	21.15	21.55	1.9	1.1	17

Source: Kirin Beer University Global Beer Production Report, 2014.

decades. From 2013 to 2014, for example, the production and consumption growth rates in the region were 0.7 percent and 3.0 percent, respectively.

Colombia lies in northwestern South America, has a population of more than 47 million people, and is the fourth largest economy in Latin America. Table 8.1 summarizes Colombia's beer production and consumption for 2013 and 2014. In economic terms, the 2014 beer consumption levels in Colombia represented a total expenditure of US$6.9 billion, which accounted for 1.8 percent of the country's US$377.7 billion GDP.[4] However, Colombians' per capita beer consumption of 46 liters per year is relatively low on a global basis,[5] and ranks below average regionally (see Figure 8.3).

Bavaria Brewery is the biggest beer manufacturer in Colombia, enjoying 98 percent market share with 18 different domestic and international brands, such as Aguila, Poker, Club Colombia, and Peroni. The remaining 2 percent of the market is mainly artisanal breweries, among which stands out Bogota Beer Company with a 1.1 percent share. Today, Bavaria owns eight plants in Colombia, including six breweries and two malting plants.[6] As Table 8.2 shows, the breweries range in production capacity from 2.3 to 10.2 million hl per year. In 2014, Bavaria sold more than 20 million hl of beer, the highest in the company's 125-year history. In that same year, Bavaria reported gross sales of US$3.14 billion, net sales of US$1.41 billion and net income of 1.30 billion.[7]

The "five worlds" approach that comprised the aforementioned PROSPERAR sustainability program enabled SABMiller to have a global and aligned strategy, while at the same time addressing local

Table 8.2 Bavaria's plants and their production numbers

Plant name	Type	Production capacity (million hl/year, 2016)	Current production (million hl/year, 2016)
Barranquilla	Brewery	4.9	4.3
Boyaca	Brewery	2.4	1.9
Bucaramanga	Brewery	2.3	1.9
Medellin	Brewery	3.5	3.1
Tocancipa	Brewery	10.2	9.6
Valle	Brewery	5.8	4.4
Tibito	Malting		
Malteria Tropical	Malting		
Total	–	29.1	25.3

Source: Bavaria.

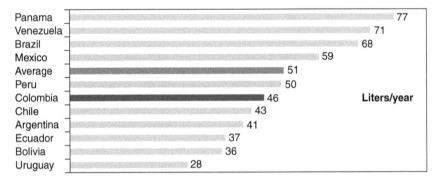

Figure 8.3 Per capita beer consumption in Latin America.

Source: Kirin Beer University Global Beer Production Report, 2014. Some values calculated by author from total national consumption figures.

needs and challenges. The execution of PROSPERAR is meant to rely heavily on partnerships. As a subsidiary of SABMiller, Bavaria abided by a set of sustainability guidelines and objectives defined at the headquarters in London, which were then grounded in the Colombian context to ensure a feasible local strategy.[8] Bavaria has continued this approach under Anheuser-Busch InBev, with each PROSPERAR "World" devoted to different social responsibility objectives.

Thriving World

The main purpose of Thriving World is to promote equity and quality of life internally, throughout Bavaria's value chain and in the communities where it operates. The program emphasizes four issues:

- inclusive growth and development in Bavaria's value chain;
- contribution to society and to the communities surrounding Bavaria facilities;
- human rights in the domestic sphere and in the supply chain; and
- occupational health, safety, and industrial hygiene.

Bavaria has launched more than 25 different initiatives under Thriving World, and reports two main key performance indicators, or KPIs: the number of small- and medium-sized businesses involved in initiatives and the percentage of employed women performing executive or managerial roles within the company. In 2015, 28.4 percent of female employees held leadership roles.[9]

Sociable World

Bavaria believes that beer is a sociable alcoholic beverage, deeply embedded in Colombia's culture, festivities, and social life. However, fully aware of the health and social issues the overconsumption of beer and other alcoholic beverages can generate, Bavaria is committed to promoting moderate, responsible, and enjoyable consumption. Sociable World defines four material issues:

- responsible and moderate alcohol consumption;
- preventing alcohol consumption in minors;
- responsible marketing; and
- preventing driving after drinking alcohol.

Bavaria's Sociable World initiatives have impacted more than 400,000 workers and consumers.[10]

Resilient World

Bavaria acknowledges that water is a strategically important resource for stakeholders and for the business itself. It uses three main KPIs to measure its commitment to preserving water resources in its internal operations as well as externally, in other operating regions:

- responsible use of water resources;
- wastewater management; and
- scarcity and water quality risk management.

Two main measures of performance are the efficiency in water use for the production of beer and soft drinks, and the percentage of water input that comes from safe water sources. Resilient World is the focus of this case study.

Clean World

Bavaria acknowledges that its operations generate waste and contribute to climate change. Through the Clean World program, it has targeted three material issues to reinforce its environmental management, develop waste reuse and recycling strategies, and reduce carbon dioxide (CO_2) emissions throughout its value chain:

- CO_2 emission reduction from productive and nonproductive activities;
- efficient waste management; and
- recycling and innovation in packaging.

Three main KPIs measure these objectives: CO_2 emissions during the production and packaging processes, the rate of material reuse and recycling, and the acquisition of green and efficient technology. Some cumulative results up to the year 2015 include a 30 percent reduction in the amount of CO_2 emitted per hl of beer produced; a 56.1 percent waste reduction from 2013 to 2014; and a 96.49 percent waste recycling rate in 2015.

Productive World

Productive World focuses on how Bavaria works with its barley and sugar suppliers to foster best practices in sustainable agriculture. To improve practices, the company is working to develop capacity-building programs for farmers and certify its sugar supply with the global non-profit Bonsucro, which works to promote sustainable sugarcane.

To show its commitment to corporate sustainability through the five worlds, Bavaria participated in the Dow Jones Sustainability Index for the first time in 2014. Earning a total score of 71 points, Bavaria received its highest marks in the environmental dimension (77), and fell just one point shy of making the Dow Jones Sustainability™ Emerging Markets Index. Other high marks include a 67 in the economic dimension and 71 in the social dimension. Bavaria scored 15 points above the global average for beer manufacturers. In addition, it carries some impressive certifications—ISO 9001, ISO 14001, OHSAS 18001, and ISO 22000[11]—further solidifying its commitment to the highest health, security, environmental, and quality standards.

Sustainability Analysis: Resilient World

In 2005, Bavaria reached a tipping point as a business and as a sustainable operation. The company's sustainability strategy flowed through two corporate streams: water use and water management. One word captures the "before" picture for Bavaria up to this point: passivity. Its environmental vision was inert and reactive, focusing only on legal and regulatory compliance. Bavaria established goals for reducing water use, but they were not as stringent as those of other companies in the beer industry. Because Colombia was known for its comparatively low water prices,[12] sensitivity to its use was rare, even nonexistent. This shallow approach would change when Bavaria merged with SABMiller, the second-largest beer company in the world. The "after" picture is an upended narrative in which Bavaria emerged as a proactive company, with a public commitment and a well-defined sustainability strategy with structured water use and management processes.

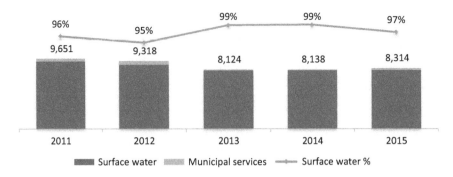

Figure 8.4 Bavaria's water consumption in thousands of m³ by source.
Source: Calculation made with figures obtained from Bavaria's 2015 Sustainability Report.

To provide a comprehensive analysis of Bavaria's water strategy, this case study covers two main dimensions of the Resilient World project: an operational perspective, discussing water use and wastewater management, and an external dimension related to scarcity and water quality.

Operational Dimension: An Eco-efficiency Approach

In the context of water, the operational dimension refers to all activities related to the use and management of water resources within the walls of Bavaria's breweries and malting plants. Since brewing beer is a water-intensive process, Bavaria has focused its strategy on water use efficiency and water treatment. From 2011 to 2015, according to the company's 2016 sustainability report, Bavaria decreased its water consumption by 13.9 percent and leveled it off at an average value of 8.2 million cubic meters (MCM) per year for 2013–15. Figure 8.4 illustrates how the company procures water from two main sources— surface water and municipal water systems. Bavaria relies heavily on the former. This preference results from the lower cost of extracting surface water, even including treatment costs during production. While the cost of surface water is consistent all over Colombia at 0.00004 cents per cubic meter (m³), the cost of water from municipal aqueducts and water treatment facilities vary geographically. In 2015, Bavaria

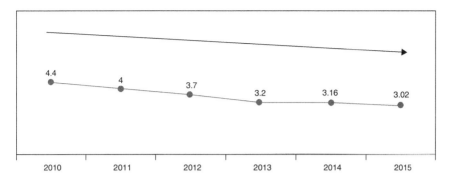

Figure 8.5 Bavaria's water consumption evolution (hl water/hl beer).

Source: Bavaria, *Sigamos Prosperando: Informe de Desarrollo Sostenible – Resumen*, 2016.

paid a total amount of US$3.37 million for the 8.314 m^3 of water it used in its operations.[13]

The most important water indicator in the beer industry is consumption, or total input of water per unit of beer produced (hl water/hl beer). According to Molson-Coors' 2015 Sustainability Report, the average ratio ranges between 3.0 and 3.5 hl of water per hl of beer produced, depending on the type of beer. From 2010 to 2015, Bavaria decreased its ratio by 31.4 percent (Figure 8.5), from 4.4 in 2010 to an impressive 3.02 in 2015[14]—a value that positions it as a more efficient brewery than its owner Anheuser-Busch InBev, Heineken, Carlsberg, Molson-Coors, and Kirin Brewery. Bavaria's 2014 water consumption ratio already exceeded Anheuser-Busch InBev's 2017 goals. Figure 8.6 illustrates the water-consumption-to-beer-production ratio for 2014 for some of the most important beer companies in the world. It indicates that Bavaria is the most efficient company, using 35.5 percent less water per beer than its competitors. But the story does not end there. When disaggregating data by each of Bavaria's breweries, some are even more efficient, with unprecedented levels that are below 3 hl of water per hl of beer. Figure 8.7 illustrates the water consumption of each of the malting and brewery plants from 2013 to 2015.

How has Bavaria achieved such efficient water consumption? The key was two processes through which Bavaria has continuously learned and challenged itself over time: recycling and culture.

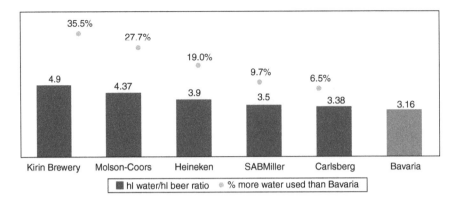

Figure 8.6 Water consumption ratio benchmark (hl water/hl beer).

Source: Constructed with water consumption values reported in each of the companies' sustainability reports for the year 2014.

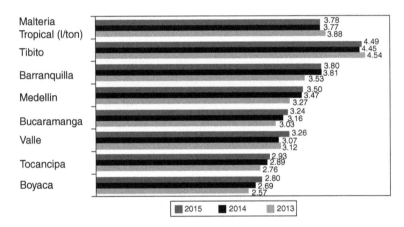

Figure 8.7 Water consumption per Bavaria plant (hl water/hl beer).

Source: Bavaria, *Sigamos Prosperando: Informe de Desarrollo Sostenible - Resumen*, 2015.

Recycling

Recycling is defined by the US Environmental Protection Agency (EPA) as "the process of collecting and processing materials that would otherwise be thrown away as trash and turning them into new products." It is considered a basic waste management concept. Conscious of recycling's importance, and driven by a set of global guidelines coming from SABMiller's headquarters, Bavaria has implemented a series of initiatives to recycle water and reuse it for other purposes. More

Table 8.3 Water consumption for 2014 and 2015

Plant	Water consumption (thousands of m³)	Water recovered (thousands of m³)	% water recovered
Tocancipa	5,294.8	948.1	18
Valle	2,433.3	97.4	4
Total	7.728.1	1045.5	14

Source: Bavaria, *Sigamos Prosperando: Informe de Desarrollo Sostenible - Resumen*, 2015.

specifically, the investment in technological upgrades at two brewery plants—Tocancipa in 2011 and Valle in 2013—enabled the company to recover 14 percent of the water consumed at both plants in 2014 and 2015 (Table 8.3). This recovered water was mainly reused for down-cycled activities such as washing floors and machinery, according to interviews conducted with Bavaria personnel.

Short-Cycle Intervals

As mentioned above, perhaps the most powerful strategy Bavaria has used to promote efficiency is the establishment of "short-cycle intervals," which have been firmly embedded in the company's operational culture, allowing the company to generate real-time information about its operations and, consequently, better control its water use. As Bavaria's director of utilities said, "People do not see these intervals as an obligatory or a compliance task; they enjoy it and it has now become a habit." The intervals are complemented by weekly area meetings at which operators are encouraged to learn about their peers' work, exchange ideas, and propose solutions to day-to-day challenges the organization faces.

Wastewater Management: Zero Fines

Until 2015, Decree 1954 governed water discharges to water bodies and sewage systems in Colombia (Figure 8.8). The regulation classified Bavaria with the "industrial category," which meant the company never had to pay a *peso* for violating any wastewater regulations. However,

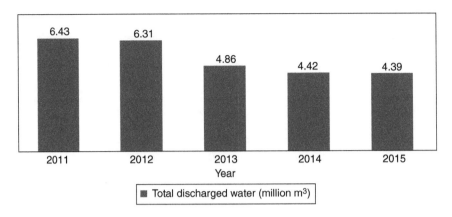

Figure 8.8 Bavaria's discharged wastewater, 2011–15.

Source: Bavaria, *Sigamos Prosperando: Informe de Desarrollo Sostenible - Resumen*, 2015.

Resolution 0631—created by the Colombian Ministry of Environment and Sustainable Development in 2015—introduced a new category for the beer industry with new rules. As a result, Bavaria is today required to meet more stringent physicochemical parameters for its water discharges such as limits on pH, biochemical oxygen demand, chemical oxygen demand, total suspended solids, phosphorous compounds, and nitrogen compounds, among others.

In addition to national compliance, guidelines from SABMiller's headquarters also required Bavaria to communicate and report one parameter in particular: the chemical oxygen demand (COD). According to the EPA, COD measures the "amount of oxygen that is required to oxidize all of the organic and inorganic compounds in a water body," which helps indicate the impact of wastewater released into aquatic ecosystems. Bavaria has reduced its volume of discharged water through the implementation of initiatives aimed at water use efficiency. In 2015, Bavaria discharged a total volume of 4.39 million cubic meters of wastewater, a 31.7 percent decrease from 2011 levels.

To comply with national and organizational guidelines, Bavaria has wastewater treatment plants in all of its production facilities except for Medellin, where wastewater is discharged and then treated in the city's San Fernando water treatment plant. Bavaria works along with the treatment plant to ensure the effluent meets all the required physiochemical parameters when it is finally discharged to superficial water bodies. Because four of its eight plants were above the maximum permissible values for COD—the Boyacá and Malteria Tropical plants exceed the norm by 200 percent—Bavaria needs to focus its efforts on complying with the new physicochemical standards.

External Dimension—a Risk Approach

The external dimension of Resilient World water sustainability practices at Bavaria consists of all of the initiatives that the company undertakes beyond its own walls. These initiatives were developed with water risk management in mind. The external dimension has two major components, Bavaria's water stewardship strategy and the Water Risk Assessment Methodology. Bavaria's water stewardship strategy resulted from a strategic partnership with the World Wildlife Fund (WWF) that started in 2011, and focuses on the sustainable management of the watersheds within the company's areas of influence. The Water Risk Assessment Methodology is a tool Bavaria uses to identify and prioritize the most pressing operational water issues. Today, these two practices allow Bavaria to focus on mitigating risks. To do this, the company promotes sustainable initiatives to reduce water impacts on aquatic ecosystems from a multidisciplinary and inter-sectorial approach.

Bavaria's Water Stewardship Strategy

The results of a first study conducted by Bavaria and WWF were compelling: 10 percent of Bavaria's surface and ground water footprint is generated within its operation and the remaining 90 percent is from elsewhere in its supply chain.[15] This conclusion, in conjunction with Bavaria's heavy reliance on surface water sources for its operations, brought the need to devise a plan to address the water risks that the business faced. As a result of this understanding, both organizations embarked on a mission to work beyond Bavaria's walls and support the natural ecosystems on which the company depended.

Bavaria relied on the WWF's expertise to design its water stewardship strategy, which is embodied in a five-step framework to

Table 8.4 Watershed programs and risks addressed

Program	Risk
1. Promoting environmental sustainability and social development	Water reputational risk
2. Improving environmental dialogue in the basin	Water normative risk
3. Protecting the watershed to ensure water security	Water physical risk

promote sustainability at the watershed level.[16] As a result, the company organized a three-program "Watershed Cooperation Plan" (Table 8.4). This intervention aims to address physical, normative, and reputational water issues related to Bavaria's operation.

The cooperation plan is executed through strategic programs for six watersheds—with a total area of more than 23,000 square kilometers (2,300,000 hectares)—from which Bavaria extracts water for its operations. The level of complexity of each watershed determines the design of the program. Variables such as water dependence, size, identification of stakeholders, and data availability are taken into consideration. Table 8.5 presents the results of this process.

While the plan and strategic programs are well structured, their magnitude and scope represent the two most important water-related challenges for Bavaria, for several reasons. First, the plan calls for the execution of strategies at watersheds all over Colombia, a vast geographical area. This scale presents serious complexities, not least of which is understanding and managing the vastly dissimilar socioeconomic, environmental, and geopolitical characteristics of each watershed region. Moreover, by seeking to play a leadership role in each watershed, Bavaria needs to interact with many different stakeholders, which in some instances are poorly defined. Once identified, each stakeholder must be guided to a common understanding of why conservation and water stewardship are essential to mitigate environmental risks and boost social and economic welfare in their region.

Second, the strategies require a long-term perspective. For Bavaria and its partners to achieve true sustainability, programs must be implemented on an ongoing basis by untiring advocates who can think

Table 8.5 Watershed complexity levels

Classification	A	B-I	B-II	C
Watersheds	Doña Maria Stream and Surata River Watershed	Upper watershed of the Chicamocha river, Upper basin of the Bogotá river	Upper watershed of the Cauca river	Magdalena river watershed
Plant	Union and Bucaramanga	Boyaca, Tocancipa, and Tibito	Valle	Barranquilla, Malteria Tropical
Size	<1.000 km²	<2.000 km²	<10.000 km²	>10.000 km²
Stakeholders	Environmental authorities and key players are well defined		Well-defined environmental authorities, but key players show a high degree of uncertainty about the extent and complexity of the contributor territory	Direct and indirect environmental authorities
Data availability	Complete	Partial	Partial and fragmented	Partial, fragmented, and heterogeneous

strategically and manage day-to-day activities. Long-term planning and execution has its own built-in challenges, given the fast pace at which senior executives and decision makers change—and their strategies with them—within organizations and local governments. The issue is exacerbated by the fact that decision makers must show results during their tenures. As a result, executives often prefer short-term goals and tangible outcomes. In this regard, it is vital for Bavaria to internalize its water stewardship strategies within its broader corporate strategy, and create mechanisms not only to ensure their continuity, but to strengthen them through time.

Finally—and most importantly—effective deployment of these strategies requires significant human and economic resources. These ambitious water ecosystem interventions demand a well-structured and technically savvy team. Today, the sustainability team at Bavaria falls short on that score. Indeed, the members of the company's sustainability team can be counted on one hand and are mainly found at the company's Bogotá headquarters. In short, the implementation of the Watershed Cooperation Plan is handled primarily by the WWF. While the partnership has proven successful, it is essential that Bavaria's top management plan for the project's continuation after the WWF consultancy ends. Ultimately, it will be up to Bavaria to ensure the successful deployment of its sustainability strategy by investing the necessary financial and human capital. Thus, it is vital that the company identify the resources to manage the cooperation plan and accomplish its goals.

Water Risk Assessment Methodology

The Water Stewardship Strategy is complemented by the Water Risk Assessment Methodology (WRAM)—a tool created by SABMiller to identify and prioritize risks related to using water for the production of beer in every country where it operates. The results for Colombia in 2014 presented no significant risks to the provision of water for any of Bavaria's eight plants. However, contingent issues about the poor quality of raw water coming into the plants forced Bavaria to temporarily suspend the strategy. Fortunately, this did not cause production to stop, thanks to quick and effective responses associated with water storage. The WRAM is conducted twice a year.

Water Funds: Investing in Ecosystem Services for Water

Bavaria also supports Water Funds as part of its stewardship strategy. As their name implies, these funds bring together different stakeholders to create an endowment for sustainable initiatives that promote source water quality at specific watersheds. Examples of such investments include conservation and restoration of forests and grasslands, promotion of silvopastoral systems (which combine forests and pastures for grazing), reforestation, and eco-tourism. Currently,

Bavaria participates as a board member in three water funds—Cauca, Bogotá, and Cucuta—and collaborates with important environmental organizations such as The Nature Conservancy and the Colombian National Natural Parks agency. In total, Bavaria has been involved in more than 20 water fund investment projects, and invested a total of US$100,000 in 2015.

Conclusion

For Bavaria, 2005 was a year of paramount importance. From a business and sustainability perspective, the merger with SABMiller catapulted Bavaria into the global beer market, and focused the company's corporate social responsibility efforts on local conditions in Colombia. This merger exemplifies how multinational corporations can share knowledge and best practices to promote sustainability around the world.

As one of the five dimensions of Bavaria's PROSPERAR sustainability strategy, Resilient World represents the company's acknowledgment that water is its most precious resource. The Resilient World water management strategy combines efficiency efforts with water risk assessment. More importantly, the positive evolution of this "world" is a reflection of the company's eagerness and ability to adapt and continuously learn by making its employees the foundation for improvement. Rather than heavily investing in technology, Bavaria has invested time and resources in thinking about better and more efficient ways to solve problems on the human level.

Moreover, Bavaria's external engagement in Colombia demonstrates its pledge to continue promoting sustainable water stewardship practices. Implementing best practices around efficiency and organizational culture has permitted the company to position itself as one of the most responsible and efficient water users in the global beer industry. However, it is important to recognize that there is always room for improvement, especially when pressures from sustainability trends, technological innovation, environmental regulations, media attention, and civic consciousness will be increasingly more demanding over time.

One final reflection: the general public in Colombia and throughout Latin America recognizes Bavaria as the giant beer company that sells Aguila, Poker, and Club Colombia, but it has little knowledge of the company's sustainability efforts and best practices. Today, people are starting to value sustainability and consider it before making purchasing decisions. Bavaria must work harder to tell its sustainability story and make sure its consumers know about the accomplishments the company has made in the environmental arena. Bavaria must go beyond the publication of sustainability reports to communicate with the public. It is time for the company to find novel ways to communicate how sustainability is embedded within its business strategy. The potential to expand that message is nearly limitless since AB InBev, the world's largest beer manufacturer, acquired Bavaria. It is the time for Bavaria to let consumers and the beer market know that rather than having a sustainability strategy, it has a sustainable business model— one that can create economic growth while also fostering social and environmental well-being.

Chapter 9

GRUPO HERDEZ TAKES THE INITIATIVE IN MEXICO'S FOOD MARKET

Fairuz O. Loutfi Olivares

Abstract

Grupo Herdez is a leading producer of shelf-stable foods in Mexico and a leader in the Mexican food market of the United States. The company has more than 9,000 employees and its 40 product categories include sauces, canned food, dairy items, and organic products. Grupo Herdez has ambitious goals for its sustainability strategy, built around two major initiatives: (1) reducing greenhouse gas (GHG) emissions at its facilities through wind power, and (2) agricultural development with the brand Aires de Campo, which provides training and certification for organic products and fair trade practices. As the company's sales of organic products grew, it found its energy footprint increasing. In response, Grupo Herdez has dedicated itself to clean energy—renewable energy sources are now being used at nearly half of the company's production facilities—and GHG emissions have been halved. This case study analyzes these initiatives in the context of Mexican energy reform, as well as the nation's nutrition and obesity crisis.

Introduction

Compañia Comercial Herdez was established in 1914 in the city of Monterrey, Nuevo León, Mexico. Ignacio Hernandez del Castillo started as sales director in 1929 and went on to purchase the company in 1941. He and his sons have built the company from a distributor of toiletries and personal hygiene products to a large multinational pro-vider of shelf-stable foods (foods that can be safely stored in a sealed container at room temperature). This case study focuses on two of the company's sustainability initiatives: its wind power generation project and its efforts to build an organic food market in Mexico. The chapter also provides an overview of the Mexican food sector as context for Grupo Herdez's sustainability strategy.

Today, Grupo Herdez is a multinational company with more than 1,500 products in more than 40 different categories sold in 17 coun-tries. The company grew substantially starting in the 1940s by diversi-fying its initial products and creating strategic alliances. In the process, Grupo Herdez became one of Mexico's leading distributors of local and international food brands as well as of its own products, which include vegetables, sauces, mole (a spicy Mexican sauce made from chili and chocolate), mayonnaise, mustard, and jams.

In the 1960s, the company created a product line of canned food under the Herdez brand. To promote the new line, Grupo Herdez sponsored a variety television show, *Domingos Herdez*, which aired nationally for 12 years and raised the company's profile considerably. Additionally, the company entered the tuna and large-scale beekeeping businesses, began pasta production, started selling frozen food, and established the MegaMex Foods company in the United States.

The mission of Grupo Herdez is "to place quality foods and beverages within the reach of consumers, under brands of growing prestige and value." The company includes sustainability as part of its vision, which it describes in a recent annual report as "to consolidate, grow and position itself as a leading company in the food and beverage industry, recognized for the quality of its products and the effectiveness of its efforts in satisfying consumers' needs and expectations, within a framework of optimal consumer care and service, under strict profit-ability criteria, strategic potential and sustainability."

Grupo Herdez has 15 factories, 12 distribution centers, 8 tuna vessels and more than 9,000 employees throughout the world. In 2015, its products generated sales of more than US $960 million (16 billion Mexican pesos), with a net income of more than US $100 million

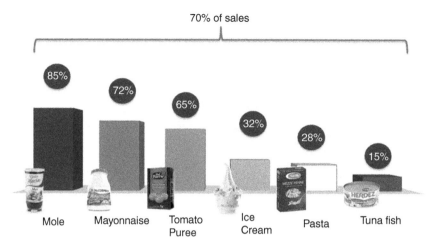

Figure 9.1 Grupo Herdez market share.
Source: Investors Relations and Sustainability Department, Grupo Herdez.

Figure 9.2 Grupo Herdez strategy.
Source: Investors Relations and Sustainability Department, Grupo Herdez.

(1,500 million Mexican pesos). The company's main markets are Mexico and the United States. The market share in Mexico of Grupo Herdez's main product categories ranges from 15 percent for tuna to 85 percent for mole (see Figure 9.1).

The corporate strategy of this multinational company consists of five core areas—organic growth, innovation, development/acquisition of infrastructure, operational efficiency, and international growth. Sustainability is the baseline for all of them, as shown in Figure 9.2, and the company's sustainability initiatives support all five strategic areas. Thus, this chapter's overview of sustainability at Herdez identifies how it helps the company's strategy of "focus[ing] on building a sustainable, responsible and profitable growth for our stakeholders, while continuously investing to maintain our strong brand awareness supported by the market knowledge we have developed over 100 years."[1]

The Best Practice

Grupo Herdez has focused on expanding the acceptance and sales of organic foods in Mexico. In 2015, the company saw record sales, with an increase of 14.2 percent over the previous year. Ironically, perhaps, the expansion into the organic market increased the company's energy consumption and greenhouse gas (GHG) emissions from its facilities. To mitigate this increased environmental impact, Grupo Herdez turned to renewable energy, its best practice. Grupo Herdez took advantage of the new electricity market in the wake of government reforms in 2013 by turning to wind power. In the process, the company found that using renewable energy made economic sense and enhanced its brand perception.

Sustainability Strategy

In recent years, sales of natural food products in Mexico have seen a sharp increase while sales of processed foods have remained steady, in part because of some national regulatory changes. In 2013, to combat obesity, the Mexican government implemented a 10 percent tax on sugar-sweetened beverages and an 8 percent tax on food items considered "junk food." The Mexican Secretariat of Health, specifically the Federal Commission for the Protection against Sanitary Risks (COFEPRIS), has also issued a new regulation for food advertising and labeling. This regulation requires food and drink manufacturers to identify the health contents of their products and include a front-of-pack nutrition label in processed packaged foods with information on sugar, sodium, fats, and caloric content per portion.[2] Grupo Herdez has incorporated the regulation into its social, economic, and environmental initiatives.

The food market in Mexico is changing. Grupo Herdez is helping drive new trends by marketing low-fat, low-sodium, and low-sugar products. Since acquiring *Aires de Campo*®, a leading manufacturer of organic products in Mexico, in 2010, Grupo Herdez has begun introducing more

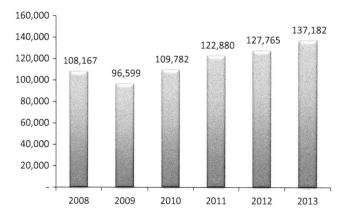

Figure 9.3 Processed food production in Mexico (million US dollars).
Source: National Institute of Statistics and Geography (INEGI), Mexico.

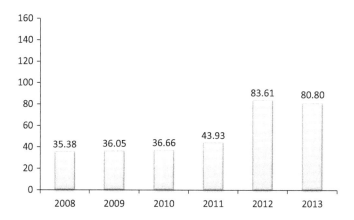

Figure 9.4 Organic food production in Mexico (million US dollars).
Source: National Institute of Statistics and Geography (INEGI), Mexico. Converted from Mexican pesos to US dollars with the foreign exchange rate from Banco de Mexico.

natural foods. Figures 9.3 and 9.4 provide an overview of processed and organic food production in Mexico from 2008 to 2013. The scale of processed food production has increased, but organic food production is also trending upward, for reasons I describe in the next section.

Worldwide, the demand for organic food products continues to grow. In Mexico, organic agriculture plays an important role in sustainable economic development. The country ranks first in global organic coffee exports and third in organic honey exports. Organic production, as stated in the Law of Organic Products published by the Mexican government, is a "system of production and processing of food, products and sub products (animal, vegetable or others) with regulated use of external supplies, restricting and banning the use of synthetic chemical products."[3]

Grupo Herdez adheres to the four principles of organic agriculture established by the International Federation of Organic Agriculture Movements (IFOAM) in 2005: *health* of individuals, communities, and ecosystems through the maintenance of physical, mental, social, and ecological well-being; *ecology* based on living ecological systems and cycles; *fairness* through equity, respect, justice, and stewardship of the planet among people and living beings; and *care* through responsible practices. IFOAM is recognized as the only international organic umbrella organization that unites stakeholders in more than 100 countries.[4] As the organics market expands, Grupo Herdez has been forced to increase its energy consumption to meet production demand. However, rather than falling back on the old paradigm of fossil fuel based energy, the company has initiated alternative energy projects to supply its needs.

The energy playing field in Mexico is not always level, though. According to the International Renewable Energy Agency (IRENA), Mexico accounts for one-fifth of all energy use in Latin America. Further, Mexico is the world's tenth-largest oil and natural gas producer.[5] Major public concerns remain about the country's continued dependence on natural gas, as well as the environmental impacts of using fossil fuels. Therefore, the federal government passed energy reforms in 2013 that have created a wholesale electricity market in an attempt to modernize the power sector, encourage lower electricity costs, and promote higher usage of cleaner technologies. The reforms also brought new opportunities for the private sector to invest in clean energy and renewable energy projects.

The concept of sustainability was first explored at Grupo Herdez ten years ago with the creation of the Corporate Social Responsibility (CSR) Committee. The establishment of this committee was in part a result of the affiliation of a board member of Grupo Herdez with the board of trustees of the Mexican Center for Philanthropy (CEMEFI),

PERIOD	2013	2014	2015	2015 GOAL
WATER — GOAL: Reduce potable water consumption by 20% compared to 2009				
m³/ton produced	3.9	3.0	3.1	2.6
reduction compared to 2009	+20%	-7%	-5%	-20%
EMISSIONS — GOAL: Reduce CO₂e emissions by 20% compared to 2010				
Ton CO₂e/ton produced	0.16	0.15	0.13	0.20
reduction compared to 2010	-38%	-42%	-49%	-20%
ENERGY — GOAL: Reduce consumption by 10% compared to 2009				
kWh/ton produced	150.9	149.5	149.4	143.0
reduction compared to 2009	-5%	-6%	-6%	-10%
GOAL: 80% of energy consumed coming from clean or alternative sources				
kWh	8,673,746	15,959,316	19,503,276	N.A.
consumption compared to 2009	15%	25%	30%	80%
WASTE — GOAL: reduce volume sent for final disposal by 20% compared to 2009				
Waste generated/ton produced	0.10	0.09	0.07	0.02
reduction compared to 2009	+345%	+320%	+209%	-20%
GOAL: increase recycled waste by 5% per year				
recycled waste	36%	42%	55%	45%

Figure 9.5 Environmental performance indicators at Grupo Herdez.
Source: Grupo Herdez Annual Report 2015.

an organization composed of more than 1,500 companies, institutions, organizations, and individuals working on social and environmental causes. It promotes philanthropic and socially responsible action from citizens, organizations, and companies to achieve a prosperous, equitable, and supportive society. One of its objectives is to increase the number of companies adopting CSR with sustainable solutions that contribute to the development of Mexico.[6]

After the creation of the CSR Committee, in 2008 and for eight consecutive years thereafter, Grupo Herdez received the Corporate Social Responsibility distinction awarded by CEMEFI. In 2009, Grupo Herdez received the Clean Industry Certificate issued by the Mexican government and in 2010 the company conducted the first environmental impact assessment of its operations, which led to the establishment of the environmental performance goals for the 2010–15 period. Since then, Grupo Herdez has measured its environmental performance by monitoring its building of green infrastructure such as energy cogeneration projects; its increasing use of clean energy and efficient use of resources; its reduction in water consumption; and its increase in recycling. In the 2012–13 period, these indicators were updated to the ones shown in Figure 9.5.

In recent years, Grupo Herdez has joined a range of global sustainability initiatives including the United Nations (UN) Global Compact, Global Environmental Management Initiative (GEMI), and the Carbon Disclosure Project (CDP). It is also member of ECOCE, an environmental nonprofit association that promotes the recycling of containers and packaging; CESPEDES, the Mexican chapter of the World Business Council for Sustainable Development (WBCSD); and SUSTENTA, the Corporate Commitment for Solid Waste Management.

Grupo Herdez has also implemented a Code of Conduct for Suppliers and added labor, environment, and human rights clauses to all its purchasing contracts. To improve its supply chain practices, it has started the first pilot project of a life-cycle assessment for one of its main products, McCormick mayonnaise. Measuring the performance of these initiatives is crucial for Grupo Herdez to realize sustainability as a strategic opportunity.

Figure 9.6 shows the full-time sustainability team at Grupo Herdez. The Investors Relations and Sustainability area is in charge of preparing sustainability reports, the external verification process, and the publication of related information. The company's information is shared with international initiatives including Global Reporting Initiative (GRI), UN Global Compact, and CDP. Figure 9.6 provides an overview of how sustainability is integrated into the organizational structure of Grupo Herdez, illustrating the direct relationship between Corporate Finance Division and Investors Relations and Sustainability. This internal structure is suitable for the implementation and monitoring of sustainability initiatives, though the finance division should be more involved in the sustainability area where it aligns with business considerations.

Sustainability has a personal dimension at Herdez too. In developing sustainability projects, the Investors Relations and Sustainability Department noticed that not all employees were familiar with sustainability terms. To raise awareness, the company started the *Tierra Herdez* campaign[7] in 2015 to educate its employees on all aspects of sustainability. This campaign provides information (e.g., definitions of sustainability and climate change, practical ways to reduce environmental impacts, etc.) that employees can use in their professional activities and

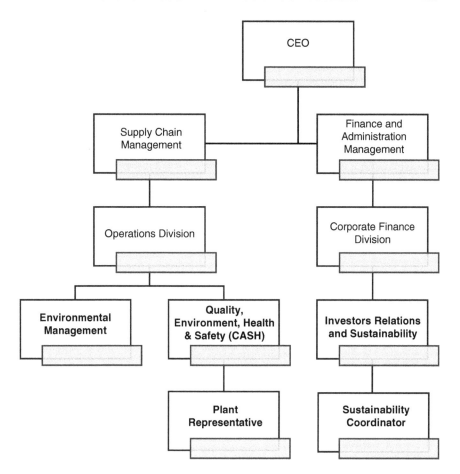

Figure 9.6 Sustainability organization chart at Grupo Herdez.

daily lives. This effort has led to an increase in productivity on the job and has facilitated collaboration and communication.

Sustainability with Organic Foods

Aires de Campo®, now owned by Grupo Herdez, was the first commercialization and distribution company for organic foods in Mexico. The company was created to connect a network of high-quality organic producers with consumers interested in healthier and more sustainable eating habits. The company currently works with 76 commercial partners and a specialized team of 61 people dedicated to producing high-quality organic food. Through *Aires de Campo*®, Grupo Herdez distributes 112 products in the following categories: groceries, dairy products, meat, eggs, and beverages. Despite a recent uptick in distribution, challenges remain. For example, the company struggles to ensure its supply of products and has had to work with suppliers to improve their skills while also seeking new providers. Other challenges involve water costs, waste management costs, and working conditions for Grupo Herdez employees.

Turning to Wind Power

In 2009, Grupo Herdez joined a wind power generation project on the Isthmus of Tehuantepec, in the state of Oaxaca, that contracted for 45,331,740 kilowatt-hours (kWh) per year. The company had decided to consider alternative energy projects such as this one, which consumed clear electricity and reduced direct GHG emissions as well as electricity costs. To monitor the progress of energy projects like this, Grupo Herdez used G4 Sustainability Reporting Guidelines from the Global Reporting Initiative (GRI), including *energy consumption within the organization (indicator EN3), energy intensity (EN5),* and *reduction of energy consumption (EN6).*[8]

The wind-generation project was developed by Électricité de France (EDF) and began operations in 2013. Currently, it supplies electricity to five of Grupo Herdez's facilities. Two of these facilities (the Industrias Plant and the Santa Rosa Plant) are the company's most important, based on volume of production (Table 9.1). Through clean energy projects like sourcing from EDF, Grupo Herdez has sought to reduce its GHG emissions. In 2015, Grupo Herdez's GHG emissions declined by 3,781 tons, representing a reduction of 7.2 percent compared to 2014.[9]

Cogeneration Project

In 2015, a cogeneration project of 4.6 megawatts (MW) was authorized for Grupo Herdez. This project supplies 70 percent of the thermal

Table 9.1 Grupo Herdez facilities that use electricity from the wind-generation project

Facility	Location in Mexico (state)	Production or operation of the facility	Wind power capacity contracted (kWh)
Chiapas Plant	Chiapas	Tuna production	8,078,482
Industrias Plant	San Luis Potosi	Mole, 8 Vegetables juice, nopal, and sauces production	5,279,749
Santa Rosa Tomates Plant	Sinaloa	Vegetables, sauces and chillies production	3,618,607
San Bartolo	Mexico City	Office building	12,045,350
Central Offices	Mexico City	Office building	848,404

Source: Investors Relations and Sustainability Department, Grupo Herdez. Mexico, 2016.

energy used by the Herdez plant in San Luis Potosi and at the same time generates electricity. It uses the electricity surplus in some of the San Luis Potosi buildings with the highest electricity costs to create a new source of income and energy savings. The cogeneration project began operating at the end of 2016. Around the same time, a new protocol was introduced—to release energy audits for each of Grupo Herdez's facilities that measure the heating and cooling requirements in each plant. If the audits find positive results for the San Luis Potosi cogeneration project, Grupo Herdez will consider similar projects for other facilities.

Sustainability Analysis

Grupo Herdez's most effective sustainability practice is the implementation of wind power generation to meet its growing energy demand. Currently, five Grupo Herdez facilities use wind energy from EDF's wind plant in Oaxaca. The plant provides 30 percent of the energy the company consumes and the facilities using wind energy represent 48 percent of Grupo Herdez's production in Mexico. The wind energy project also saved the company money in the 2012–13 period. At that time, the cost of wind power electricity generation was 10 percent lower than the cost of electricity from fossil fuels provided by the state-run Federal Commission of Electricity (CFE) utility company. Additionally, carbon dioxide (CO_2) emissions were reduced by 49 percent compared to 2010, surpassing Grupo Herdez's target of a 20 percent CO_2 emissions reduction by 2015.[10]

Since 2013, however, electricity rates have changed, creating new challenges for the company. First, Mexico's federal government implemented a subsidy scheme that makes the cost of electricity from fossil fuels lower than the cost of electricity from clean energy sources such as wind or solar. Since 2015, according to Grupo Herdez, electricity from wind energy has become 15 percent more expensive than electricity from fossil fuels.[11] Because of this increased cost, plant managers at Grupo Herdez prefer electricity from the grid.

Second, implementation challenges have made it difficult for the company to start some ambitious energy projects. For example, the San Luis Potosi cogeneration project was expected to be an effective alternative for the company to reduce costs, fuel consumption, and CO_2 emissions. However, these types of projects were internally evaluated based on a cost-benefit analysis for the short, medium, and long term, and the company has to decide whether to authorize them. Also, Grupo Herdez must take new legislation and regulatory requirements in Mexico into consideration, adding time to the decision-making process. According to the new regulations, clean energy projects require additional permits from regulatory and energy agencies, including the Secretariat of Energy (SENER), the CFE, the Regulatory Energy Commission (CRE), and the National Commission for the Efficient Use of Energy (CONUEE).

The wind energy project is Grupo Herdez's most effective sustainability practice based on its environmental performance indicators. Considering the current initial status of energy reform in Mexico, it can also be expected that the cost of electricity from renewable sources will decrease in the future, at which point the company will save money.

Grupo Herdez's sustainability initiatives still have room for improvement. In particular, the company should look for other electricity sources in order to meet the ambitious target of *80% of energy consumed coming from clean or alternative sources.*

Sustainability Targets

One important strategy for Grupo Herdez as it strengthens its sustainability initiatives is to review them periodically and adjust targets. After all, in 2015, it had not reached some of the targets it set earlier (shown in Figure 9.5). Each of the company's plants establishes its own environmental targets based on annual performance and previously implemented projects. These targets are then evaluated every five years, focusing on the company's main indicators: water, waste, energy, and emissions reduction. Since 2009, Grupo Herdez has measured its GHG emissions. Since 2011, the company has reported the measurements to GEI Mexico, a national voluntary program to track GHGs.

In 2015, the company achieved its emissions reduction target. However, new challenges continue to arise. Reduction of potable water consumption, for example, has been difficult due to the company's constant need for water. The company is working to address this challenge by installing three rainwater collection and storage systems, which recycled or reused 4 percent of the total volume of water collected in 2015. In terms of energy, the company increased its renewable energy use in recent years, as described above, and reported that 30 percent of the energy it consumed came from clean or alternative sources. Figure 9.5 shows the details of each environmental performance indicator per year since 2013 and the values reached by 2015.

Other Challenges

Grupo Herdez has faced other internal and external challenges in the implementation of some of its sustainability initiatives. Internal challenges include a lack of knowledge about sustainability initiatives or cost reduction priorities. External challenges include a lack of

Table 9.2 Internal and external challenges in the implementation of sustainability initiatives at Grupo Herdez

Internal challenges	External challenges
Alignment of objectives among different responsible areas	Mexican consumers still do not demand information about sustainability in the supply chain of products
Little employee knowledge about sustainability and its implications	Few suppliers in Mexico that can provide professional advice on sustainability issues
Lack of interest in certain operational areas	Unions and the influence of political parties are a major factor in agricultural development programs
Difficulty of implementing new projects	Sectorial working groups tend to focus on social responsibility initiatives and not sustainability initiatives
Cost reduction is a priority in all areas, limiting the implementation of sustainable projects in operation	There are not enough incentives to migrate to renewable energy
Cost reduction of fossil fuels has increased their consumption	Government programs to improve labor conditions are very complex and none have enough support from any federal entity

Source: Investors Relations and Sustainability Department, Grupo Herdez, 2016.

incentives from the government and insufficient sustainability expertise. Specific challenges are listed in Table 9.2.

After identifying its current challenges, Grupo Herdez has been looking at ways to overcome them. The previously mentioned *Tierra Herdez* campaign is an example of an effort to increase employee engagement in sustainability. It has also helped solve other internal challenges, such as a lack of employee interest in certain operational areas and difficulty implementing new projects. External challenges are usually beyond the control of the company. However, some can be tackled by the current strategies of Grupo Herdez. For example, the company is introducing organic food to new markets and consumers. By publicizing this work and all of its sustainability initiatives among suppliers, customers, and other companies in the food sector in Mexico,

Grupo Herdez can raise awareness of sustainability issues and needs in the country.

Conclusion

Sustainability is becoming a more common focus for companies in Mexico and Latin America. Following this trend, Grupo Herdez has substantially increased its focus on sustainability initiatives in recent years, and has achieved dramatic reductions in its energy footprint through the use of wind power. The company will continue to establish ambitious targets for the next five years and focus on eliminating waste, reducing emissions, and decreasing water consumption as well as using more energy from clean or alternative sources. Although some of the company's sustainability initiatives have not been as successful as expected, Grupo Herdez is committed to solving internal challenges and seeking alternatives for external ones. Because the company is continuously expanding its operations, the reduction of waste and water consumption in particular will be an ongoing challenge.

Two key future sustainability goals for the company are the continued reduction of electricity consumption and CO_2 emissions. Achieving these goals will require collaboration from all areas of the company as well as better incentives from Mexico's regulatory authorities. Although challenges persist, Grupo Herdez is on the right track toward finding the best solutions with a triple bottom line approach of economic, environmental, and social value.

Chapter 10

CHILE'S LAS PALMAS AVOCADO ORCHARD: WATER CONSUMPTION REDUCTION IN AGRICULTURE

Siegfried King

Abstract

This case study reviews the best sustainable water use practices of the Las Palmas avocado orchard, located in the Aconcagua valley of central Chile. Although this fertile agricultural region sits in the heart of Chile's wine country, it has suffered from drought in recent years. As food demand continues to grow in a world with more than seven billion people, food producers in Chile and around the world need to improve their stewardship of water resources. Las Palmas exemplifies a host of water-saving strategies, including high-density planting, crop selection, and soil moisture sensors to control precision irrigation. The implementation of these sustainable practices allows a water-dependent orchard to increase competitiveness, reduce operational costs, mitigate risk, and add value to products.

Introduction

According to the United Nations, 70 percent of global water withdrawals are linked to food and agriculture.[1] Everything that we eat needs water to survive and grow. The stress on water resources will only get worse as global population increases and demand for food rises. Economic development will also increase the demand for fruits and vegetables, such as

---

Jorge Schmidt, Las Palmas's owner, is the author's father-in-law.

Table 10.1 Planted surface of Jorge Schmidt's companies, 2015

Planted surface (acres)	Avocado	Tangerine	Table grape	Wine grape
Desarrollo Agrario S.A.	618	222	593	–
Jorge Schmidt y Cia. Ltda.	1,483	741	57	74
Agricola Alto Aconcagua Ltda.	741	–	–	–
Total	2,842	964	650	74
Total fruit-planted acres	4,529			

Source: Information provided to the author by Las Palmas by email February 1, 2016.

avocados, tangerines, and grapes, that will, in turn, require more water to produce. One Chilean company is working to address this challenge by reducing the amount of water it needs to grow avocados.

This case study will focus on the best sustainable water use practices of the Las Palmas avocado orchard. Located in the fertile Aconcagua valley, 60 miles north of Chile's capital Santiago, Las Palmas comprises 1,972 acres of fruit-producing trees, including tangerines, table grapes, wine grapes, and avocados. Avocados account for half of the orchard's planted surface. In recent years, the surrounding valley has suffered from periods of prolonged drought. This chapter will show how the company has implemented initiatives to save water and provide environmental, social, and economic benefits.

The Jorge Schmidt y Compañía Limitada, founded by Jorge Schmidt in 1986, owns Las Palmas, other orchards, and two other agricultural companies in the area—Desarrollo Agrario S.A. and Agricola Alto Aconcagua Ltda. These three companies combined employ more than 1,650 people and manage upward of 4,500 acres of productive agricultural plantations. The companies grow avocados, tangerines, and grapes (see Table 10.1).

The group focuses on premium quality fruit for export. Last year, the three companies combined produced more than 100 million pounds of fruit, generating revenues of US$45 million in exports to markets in the United States, Europe, and Asia. Table 10.2 shows the production levels and the main market for each fruit.[2] The largest of Schmidt's holdings is Las Palmas, comprising nearly 2,000 fruit-producing acres (see Table 10.3).

Table 10.2 Jorge Schmidt's companies' yearly production and markets

Fruit	Yearly production		Main export market
	in million lbs	in million kg	
Avocado	44.1	20	Europe
Tangerine	35.3	16	North America
Table grape	19.8	9	Southeast Asia
Total	99.2	45	

Source: Information provided to the author by Las Palmas by email February 1, 2016.

Table 10.3 Las Palmas's planted surface

Planted surface (acres)	Avocado	Tangerine	Table grape	Wine grape
Las Palmas	988	741	57	185
Total fruit-planted acres	1,972			

Source: Information provided to the author by Las Palmas by email February 1, 2016.

That planted surface and its substantial yields make Las Palmas an important player within the Chilean avocado industry. In 2012, Chile produced 814 million pounds of avocados and exported 210 million pounds. The country ranks second worldwide in both avocado production and avocado exports. (Mexico is first in both categories.) As shown in Table 10.2, in 2015, Schmidt's companies produced more than 44 million pounds of avocados for export.

The overall export fruit industry in Chile is much broader. The country is the main fruit exporter of the southern hemisphere. With over 750,000 acres of planted area, the Chilean fruit industry produces 11 billion pounds of produce each year, 52 percent of which is exported. This represents a US$4 billion per year industry.[3] The avocado industry has been growing to meet worldwide demand. As of 2013, 4.5 million tons of avocados were harvested commercially worldwide, and over a million tons were traded internationally. This international trade represents an annual business of over US$2 billion.

No matter how fertile their soil or how sunny the climate, however, all of these fruits need water to survive and flourish. Avocados are a water-intensive fruit, above average compared to other fruits in the amount

Table 10.4 Main avocado-producing countries

Ranking	Country	Production (in 1,000 tons)	Share (%)
1	Mexico	1,264	28
2	Chile	369	8
3	Dominican Republic	295	7
	Other	2,505	57
	Total	4,433	100

Source: Freshplaza.com.

Table 10.5 Main avocado-exporting countries

Ranking	Country	Exports (in 1,000 tons)	Share (%)
1	Mexico	494	46
2	Chile	95	9
3	Peru	89	8
	Other	392	37
	Total	1,070	100

Source: Freshplaza.com.

Table 10.6 Main avocado-importing countries

Ranking	Country	Imports (in 1,000 tons)	Share (%)
1	USA	503	47
2	Netherlands	96	9
3	France	95	9
	Other	388	35
	Total	1,082	100

Source: Freshplaza.com.

of water they need to ripen. According to statistics from the Food and Agricultural Organization of the United Nations FAOSTAT database, the global average water footprint of avocados is 1,981 cubic meters per ton. This is greater than the footprints of cherries (1,604), apples (822), strawberries (347) and watermelon (235) but less than those of soybeans (2,145), olives (3,015) and coffee (15,897).

It makes both environmental and business sense to adopt measures that lower the amount of water that avocados need to grow to maturity.

Tables 10.4, 10.5, and 10.6[4] show the main global avocado producers, exporters, and importers. Chile is the second largest producer and exporter. If a growing world population is to sustainably consume avocados, water use efficiency will be essential.

The Best Practice

Las Palmas is taking important steps to reduce its water consumption, including high-density planting, crop selection, and soil moisture sensors to control precision irrigation. But the orchard is a small fish in the big pond of fruit industry. A larger commitment from the whole fruit industry will be needed to fully address the water issues that the world faces. Hopefully, examples like Las Palmas can show that growing more sustainably is not only possible, but profitable as well.

The Local Water Context

Over the past 20 years, Chile's central region, which includes the Aconcagua valley, has been hit by five droughts. A significant portion of the country's avocado producers are located here. These avocado farmers mostly rely on the Aconcagua River to meet their water needs. The 214-kilometer-long river starts in the Andes and flows into the Pacific Ocean, crossing Chile from east to west. It is the main river of the broader Valparaíso region, providing 70 percent of the area's water resources.

Agriculture is the main industry in the Aconcagua valley and approximately 70 percent of water rights are allocated to agriculture. Mining and industry account for 20 percent, and drinking water makes up the remaining 10 percent. For all these stakeholders, water is essential. Many explanations for the frequency of the recent droughts exist: natural intermittency between rainy and dry years, climate change, overconsumption of water by local users, and lack of infrastructure to access water resources. What seems clear to all is that water can no longer be taken for granted, and stakeholders must use sustainable practices so that these three sectors can continue to rely on the Aconcagua River as their main water source.

Las Palmas's Sustainability Strategy

Las Palmas was designed around best practices in sustainability, based in part on successful testing in Schmidt's two other agricultural companies. Each of the orchard's social responsibility initiatives provides social, environmental, and economic benefits. Some focus more clearly on social dimensions, such as increasing workers' safety conditions, providing employment opportunities for marginalized groups, or enhancing workers' financial stability. A second set of initiatives provide environmental benefits, such as reducing water consumption, decreasing chemical use, and preventing soil erosion.

In addition to the economic benefits, these sustainability initiatives have enhanced the reputation of Schmidt's companies and led to awards at the national and international level. For example, in 2011, the British multinational retailer Marks & Spencer awarded the Sustainable Innovation Award to his Desarrollo Agrario company. John Dixon, executive director of foods for Marks & Spencer, said the prize was awarded "for their unique commitment to the community, their focus on new technology and sharing of ideas and their innovation and commitment towards building a business for the future."

Sustainability Analysis

This section introduces some of Las Palmas's specific sustainability initiatives and analyzes their social, environmental, and economic impacts.

Year-Round Work

Highly trained and engaged employees are key to producing premium quality fruit. But in an industry so marked by seasons, retaining a workforce can be a challenge, and temporary employment is a common practice. A volatile workforce can be costly due to the need for retraining, loss of talent, and low employee engagement. From the workers' perspective, intermittent work generates fluctuations in income, discontinuous health insurance coverage, and stress related to uncertain work opportunities.

The three fruits that Las Palmas produces (avocados, tangerines, and grapes) overlap in terms of seasonal workload. This means it can employ workers year-round, providing financial stability. In return, Las Palmas gets highly committed employees who work according to the company's standards on sustainability and other issues.

High-Density Planting

Historically, the standard practice for avocado orchards in Chile has been to have big trees with enough separation to allow generous growth. Instead, Las Palmas's trees are planted in a highly dense eight foot by eight foot layout, with a tree every eight feet in any direction. With this type of configuration, mature trees are much smaller than those on traditional orchards. When a tree grows, the leaves and branches consume a significant amount of water, so smaller trees use less water and allow the orchard to irrigate more efficiently. The amount of water that the ranch consumes is also closely linked to the chemicals and energy that the company uses. This means that by addressing its water consumption, the ranch has been able to reduce its operational costs as well.

In addition to the environmental benefits, this high-density design also provides social advantages. Because high-density planting often means smaller avocado trees, it eliminates the need for ladders to climb and pick the fruit, enhancing worker safety. The harvesting process demands less physical effort from workers, allowing employees who might not otherwise be able to find a job to enter the workforce. Dense planting also has a positive financial impact on the workers. Because they get paid based on the amount of fruit they pick, the more compact high-density planting arrangement allows workers to harvest more fruit per day.

Reduction of Chemical Use

Las Palmas is not an organic farm, so it uses chemicals for some applications. However, the company is committed to using them responsibly and only when strictly necessary. Pablo Aranda, CEO of Jorge Schmidt y Compañía Limitada, explained, "Reducing environmental impact on the farm and reducing reliance on chemical interventions is very important to the company for environmental and economic reasons."[5] To help reduce pesticide use, the orchard uses plague-monitoring techniques and introduces natural predators, in addition to its high-density planting. Reviewing rootstock choice has also brought benefits to the company. Switching rootstock has allowed the company to reduce the use of nitrogen by 50 percent, with associated reductions in other fertilizers.

Irrigation Technologies

Technology-aided initiatives also optimize water and chemical use. Las Palmas applies fertilizer through its irrigation system, which measures and calculates the amount of water and chemicals that each plant needs. With this strategy, Las Palmas avoids excessive use of chemicals and water. Furthermore, the company has invested in state-of-the-art energy-efficient irrigation technology, procuring only from best-in-class vendors and adhering to a strict maintenance program. These standards ensure that equipment works efficiently, preventing leakages and downtimes.

Pumping Stations

For irrigation purposes, Las Palmas has established multiple stations where water tanks and pumps are installed. At every station, these pumps distribute the water horizontally and additional pumps bring the water up to the next station. The horizontal pumps distribute water through pipelines and the system uses gravity to irrigate hills 250 feet below that pump. Re-impulsion pumps convey the rest of the water to the next station. There the configuration is the same, so those additional 250 feet of orchard are gravity-irrigated and the re-impulsion pumps send water to the next station, until the water reaches the last station. In orchards that only install one tank at the top of a hill, all the water needs to be pumped up. This means that even the trees that are located three feet above the water level are irrigated by water that was elevated to the top of the hill. The pumping layout at Las Palmas is more energy efficient than single tank systems, because water is only elevated 250 feet before gravity brings it back down.

Drip Irrigation

The Las Palmas watering system relies on drip irrigation, in contrast with irrigation systems where the water is sprayed or sprinkled. Of all the irrigation technologies and techniques that have been developed, drip irrigation uses water most efficiently. Each drop is directly delivered to the soil at the base of each tree, preventing water evaporation and waste. As I mentioned above, Las Palmas also measures and controls the amount of water it applies through this system.

Pipeline Design and Instrumentation

The Las Palmas pipeline network is engineered to bring enough water to every corner of the orchard, with one large main pipeline and many smaller secondary pipes. The installation has many valves that can be controlled remotely, allowing the operator to irrigate crop sections independently according to the water needs of each section.

The irrigation system is designed to only use the exact amount of water that the avocados need. Avocados are one of the most water-sensitive fruits—lack or excess of irrigation damages the tree and its fruit. As mentioned above, soil moisture sensors automatically measure water levels next to the trees' roots and then the pipeline system regulates water flow accordingly. Moisture sensors are installed close to the roots of the trees—at depths of 12, 24, and 36 inches. This set of depths provides information about the profile of water percolation. The sensors are installed for each unique soil zone at the orchard. The soil conditions vary significantly in a plantation of nearly 2,000 acres like Las Palmas. Sandy soils behave differently than soils where clay is the main component. In fact, when clay is present, the system may only irrigate once a week, whereas it usually irrigates every day in areas where sand conditions are predominant. These varying rates demonstrate the sustainability value of precise water management.

Another key aspect of water stewardship is preventing leakages. The pipeline system automatically measures water pressure to determine whether the pipelines are tight or if there is a leak in the system. If pressure gauges detect a drop in the inner pressure of a pipeline, an alarm is activated and a member of the maintenance team can check a monitor to find out which sensor is activating the alarm. The staff can then go to that sector of the plantation and perform a visual inspection of the pipeline to find the possible leak or the cause of the pressure drop.

Finally, flow measurements provide great insights for immediate and future operation of the irrigation system. As a short-term advantage, operators know exactly how much water the system is using. An operator can then override the system, irrigating differently than the default if necessary. For example, if the weather forecast calls for many rainy days, the operator might decide to irrigate less to avoid over-irrigation. Since the system is operated wirelessly and online, the operator can perform this task offsite.

Other Initiatives

Soil erosion occurs when streambeds are not well designed. At Las Palmas, the streambeds are strengthened by placing rocks along the sides. When heavy rains come, the beds can handle the excess water without degrading the soil next to the stream.

More generally, every plantation that the company starts must complete an Environmental Impacts Declaration (DIA in Spanish) showing that the project complies with current Chilean environmental standards. These regulations include considerations regarding biota present in the area. At Las Palmas, many native palm trees were present in the field before the plantation project started. Today, those palm trees still stand. In addition, the company kept other flower-intensive trees in place. Keeping these native trees and flowers is essential for the bees that pollinate the avocado, citrus, grape orchards, and vines.

Reducing Water Consumption: Partnerships and Research

Las Palmas is able to reduce water consumption by approaching the challenge from many perspectives. The orchard was designed to minimize water needs. The irrigation system and its layout are also important. Now that the ranch is planted, operational best practices also come into play. Additionally, the company is constantly investing in R&D and partnerships to maintain a state-of-the-art plantation.

Some of these best practices have been developed within the company. Other initiatives have been implemented because they have proven to be best practices worldwide. Las Palmas recognizes the need to keep up with developments and improvements as they become available. To do so, Las Palmas officials visit their international customers to learn what the markets are demanding. They participate in fruit conferences around the world, such as the Fruit Logistica Fair held each year in Berlin.

As part of its R&D strategy, Las Palmas works closely with educational institutions both locally and internationally, including Pontificia Universidad Católica de Valparaíso, and the University of California-Riverside. The company not only keeps a steady communication flow with these institutions, it also implements pilot tests of the latest research and allocates acreage to experimentation with new ideas regarding high-density planting, irrigation techniques, pollination, and so forth.

Conclusion

Jorge Schmidt's companies have found a way to align sustainable practices with a quality-oriented vision of their businesses. In agriculture, sustainability is intertwined with quality, and the Las Palmas case shows that best practices in sustainability can be profitable, especially when these initiatives are included during plantation design. Las Palmas uses various instruments to evaluate how its sustainability initiatives are performing and reacts promptly if data indicates to do so. The plantation has also benefited from the experience that its two sister companies had already accumulated.

The senior management at Las Palmas has been able to identify the "sweet spot" where being more sustainable means being more profitable. Many sustainability initiatives also address several economic or sustainability challenges at once. For example, energy efficiency measures pay off quickly in a country with expensive electricity like Chile. In addition, the strong link between energy and water explains why most reduced water consumption efforts translate to energy-efficient outcomes. From a social perspective, measures to reduce water use also improve the working conditions and salary of Las Palmas workers.

The company reports that many of the sustainability measures it developed and implemented have had a relatively quick payback period. However, some of the initiatives need more time to become profitable. For those cases, the company benefits from being a privately owned business, allowing it to take a longer view without the pressure of quarterly reports to shareholders. Of course, the company focuses on return on investment, but it also wants to remain in business long into the future. Sustainable practices have allowed Las Palmas to gain respect from its workforce as well as the recognition of the fruit industry and customers. The company benefits from highly committed workers, loyal customers, and awards it has won in the industry.

The selection of a region for growing a specific fruit depends on water availability, but also on many other factors. Climate conditions, soil characteristics, surrounding infrastructure, and the availability of a skilled workforce are only some of the other issues that growers consider before entering into business. Furthermore, water resources are variable, so even regions with adequate water reserves can undergo periods of stress. California is a case in point. The state has long had a productive agricultural industry, and yet it has been challenged in recent years by a drought of historic dimensions. Despite these difficulties, it's unlikely that California growers will find a "new" San Joaquin Valley to grow their fruits, or a "new" Napa Valley to plant their vineyards.

In Chile, the Aconcagua valley is similarly blessed with excellent agricultural conditions. Indeed, the climate is so similar that the region grows the same varieties of fruits and vegetables as California, including vines, table grapes, tangerines, and avocados. And, like

California, the Chilean valley has also been challenged by droughts. These dry conditions, along with overconsumption and lack of infrastructure, have caused water shortages. To overcome these challenges, it is imperative that individuals, organizations, companies, and countries start using water more sustainably.

Like any other major economic activity, agriculture causes positive and negative externalities. It is perhaps inherently more sustainable than other extractive industries like mining, but companies still have several reasons to address negative externalities such as intensive use of water and chemicals. Many of the best practices used to improve sustainability also improve operational efficiency. This overlap means that being sustainable saves money for agricultural companies. Second, by operating sustainably, companies can maintain their access to high-demand markets abroad, many of which are tightening their regulations and catering to informed customers who care about the sustainability of the products they buy.

Another aspect of sustainability for companies to consider is the relationship they build with the local communities where they operate. Being sustainable will help companies to keep their "social license to operate"[6] within communities that are increasingly aware of the impacts of the economic activities that are taking place in their proximity. In short, sustainability helps companies to maintain their activities for decades to come, without damaging the environment that allows them to run a profitable business in the first place. Las Palmas has found success by seeing sustainability as an opportunity, and businesses around the world can follow their example.

Chapter 11

MABESA: INCREASING GLOBAL COMPETITIVENESS WITH ECO-FRIENDLY DISPOSABLE PRODUCTS

Margarita Heredia Soto

Abstract

This case study illustrates how an innovative eco-friendly idea can help companies in industries with negative environmental reputations. Mabesa, a Mexican company that made and marketed disposable personal hygiene products, entered a challenging niche market with its Bio Baby diapers, establishing a unique, hard-to-copy product that was substantially more eco-friendly than its competitors. As a result, the company gained greater market share in the *premium* disposable baby diaper market in Mexico and the United States. The case highlights how even in an industry known for high pollution (the widespread use of disposable diapers comes at high environmental cost), companies can reduce the footprint of products, benefitting the environment, consumers, and businesses.

Introduction

This case study focuses on Grupo P.I. Mabe (*Productos Internacionales Mabe S.A. de C.V.*), better known as Mabesa, a Mexican company that

---

This chapter reflects Mabesa's work on Bio Baby diapers up until 2016, when Mabesa was acquired by the Belgian company Ontex. It has been written in collaboration with Richard Halbinger-Carmona, Mexico general manager of Ontex and marketing manager at Mabesa at the time of the case.

has manufactured and marketed diapers and other personal hygiene products for the past 40 years. Over that time, Mabesa established itself as one of the leading diaper makers in Latin America, rivaling multi-national corporations like Kimberly-Clark and Procter & Gamble. In 2015, Mabesa was Mexico's leading manufacturer of private-label products for disposable baby diapers, disposable adult diapers, and women's sanitary pads. In the same year, Mabesa ranked second in sales of disposable diapers for babies and adults in Mexico, Central America, Spain, and Portugal.

And yet, there is another side to this coin. Environmentalists have long criticized the diaper industry for its wastefulness. For example, *93 billion disposable diapers are discarded worldwide each year.* Further, approximately 5 percent of global solid waste is comprised of disposable diapers and other similar hygiene products. Diapers clog landfills—or even worse, they are treated as litter and tossed in ditches, rivers, lakes, or the ocean. Even those that make it into landfills require as long as 300 years to fully decompose because of the large amount of petroleum-based plastics used in their manufacture.[1]

As such alarming environmental news has increasingly become a part of consumers' decision-making processes, Mabesa officials realized that they had a significant role to play in addressing this problem. With world population surpassing 7.4 billion in 2016, the demand for diapers is only increasing. To address this problem, Mabesa turned to the "premium" niche market. Premium diapers have typically justified their higher cost by eliminating some of the chemical-laden material found in cheaper disposable diapers, in addition to absorbing more fluid (thus lasting longer), and fitting more comfortably. This chapter explains how Mabesa was able to leverage this premium diaper market in order to successfully market a more sustainable product. It begins by highlighting the best practice Mabesa offers to other companies, then lays out the firm's roots, explains the "Bio Baby" eco-friendly diaper development process and launch, highlights the strengths of Mabesa's approach to sustainability, and lays out areas for future improvement.

Mabesa's Best Practice

Mabesa advanced sustainability by creating a groundbreaking eco-friendly product in an industry that didn't previously emphasize environmental concerns. It also engaged in broader efforts to promote sustainability within and beyond the business. The company introduced the Bio Baby brand into the premium diaper market in 2007, thereby replacing much of the polyethylene and polypropylene plastics in traditional diapers with biodegradable alternatives that fully decompose in around seven years. Mabesa also infused the diaper's fibers with natural essential oils (such as chamomile and lavender) for skin protection. These innovations gave Bio Baby a unique position as the first "eco-friendly" diaper in Latin America (see Table 11.1). With this new product, the company gained greater market share in the premium market in Mexico and the United States.

Mabesa's Market Position

Mabesa began operations in 1977, headquartered in Puebla, Mexico's fourth-largest city, located 83 miles southeast of Mexico City and 170 miles west of Veracruz, a major port on the Gulf of Mexico. The company initially made and marketed only women's sanitary pads, but branched out into diapers for infants and adults in 1979. The products are now available in more than 40 countries worldwide. In 2016, the company was acquired by the Belgian company Ontex, and its name was changed to Mabe-Ontex, and then Ontex.

   In 2006, a year before the Bio Baby brand was released, the Mexican premium diaper market was dominated by Huggies, a Kimberly-Clark brand. Kimberly-Clark is a global, publicly traded company with abundant resources, which made it difficult for other companies to compete against it in production, promotion, and advertising. Mabesa was smaller than Kimberly-Clark and had a more limited budget, but the company had a good track record for innovation. It had a solid foundation in research and development, as evidenced by its portfolio of patents (240 patents in 12 countries, with 90 more

Table 11.1 Comparison between traditional diaper and Bio Baby

	Traditional diaper	Bio Baby
Packaging	Polyethylene Biodegradability: >300 years	Oxo-biodegradable Polyethylene Biodegradability: 3–6 years
Backsheet	Polypropylene Biodegradability: >300 years	Oxo-biodegradable Polyproylene Biodegradability: 3–6 years
Topsheet	Polypropylene Biodegradability: >300 years	Polypropylene/PLA 50% less petrochemicals
Leg cuffs	Polypropylene Biodegradability: >300 years	Oxo-biodegradable Polyproylene Biodegradability: 3–6 years
Transfer layer	Polypropylene Biodegradability: >300 years	100% PLA Biodegradability: 3–6 years
Impermeable liner	Polyethylene Biodegradability: >300 years	Oxo-biodegradable Polyproylene Biodegradability: 3–6 years
Super absorbent	Synthetic (acrylic acid) Not biodegradable	Synthetic+natural 20% biodegradable with less petrochemicals
Fluff	100% biodegradable	100% biodegradable

Source: Mabesa.

patents in progress), and an ability to protect its innovations from theft and replication.

The premium diaper market is profitable because it attracts higher-income consumers and has few competitors. In 2006, premium diapers comprised 25 percent of the national diaper market. The top-selling brands in Mexico's premium market were Huggies and Procter & Gamble's Pampers. Only four other companies had introduced premium diapers in Mexico at the time and without much success, partly due to the fact that their premium diapers looked too similar to existing products. Though introduced at lower prices, they had no competitive advantage and no brand positioning. Huggies and Pampers were still perceived as higher-quality products.

At that time, all of Mabesa's products were marketed only to the mid- and low-price market sectors. However, its products in these sectors were comparable to that of its larger international competitors. Within the mid-price market, representing 35 percent of the total diaper sales in Mexico, Mabesa sold the brands Champs (0.6 percent of total diaper sales) and Kiddies (3.3 percent); Kimberly-Clark sold the brands Suavelastic (21.1 percent) and Comodisec (6.8 percent); and Procter & Gamble sold Pampers (6.2 percent). Within the low-price sector, which accounted for 37 percent of the total diaper market in Mexico, Mabesa sold the brands Classic (5.5 percent) and Childs (0.2 percent) while selling another 7.3 percent on private labels; Kimberly-Clark sold the brand Kleen Bebé Absorsec (12.6 percent), and Procter & Gamble sold Pampers Basico (1.2 percent).

Mexico's Sustainability Landscape

Mabesa's increasing attention to environmentally friendly products come alongside shifts in the Mexican sustainability landscape. One of the main sustainability challenges facing Mexico has been its failure to incorporate environmental concerns into government social and economic development planning. Natural resources and ecosystem conservation efforts have also been hampered by a vicious cycle of poverty, natural resource depletion, and environmental degradation.

Balancing the environment and sustainable development requires careful management of Mexico's long-term public policies. Mexico's federal government finally officially acknowledged this fundamental principle in its 2012 National Development Plan. The plan, guided by the principle of environmental sustainability, significantly improved coordination between government agencies. Before making decisions on public policies and investments of public funds, the government now takes their environmental impact and risks into consideration, and prioritizes the efficient use of natural resources. Also, in 2011, the Mexican Stock Exchange (BMV for its initials in Spanish) launched its Sustainability Index. This index, formed by 28 qualifying companies, evaluates its participants on three criteria: management and use of natural resources, social responsibility, and corporate governance.

However, Mexico did not have much of a recycling industry in 2011, and some communities completely lacked sanitary landfills. Because of these realities, "biodegradable" was an important distinction for products. Most Mexican people understand the concept of biodegradability more readily than sustainability. The move to sustainability will require a massive public-awareness campaign aimed at consumers.

This increased emphasis on biodegradability and sustainability created an opportunity for Mabesa, since the company had prioritized the environment even before developing Bio Baby. Starting in 2002, Mabesa had been granted the Clean Industry Certification by the Mexican Federal Office for Environmental Protection (PROFEPA) for having satisfactorily complied with environmental law. Because of such sustained commitment to the environment, the company's suppliers also sought the Clean Industry Certification for their processes.

As environmental consciousness in Mexico grew, Mabesa took it further by designing and manufacturing innovative products for consumers and developing a sustainable business strategy. Though the company did not have a specialized department devoted to sustainable development, it did have a dedicated corporate social responsibility team. Because reducing the company's environmental impact was vital to Mabesa, in 2006 the company made a commitment to the following:

- Producing eco-friendly products by using more sustainable or biodegradable raw materials. All of Mabesa's products used cellulose fiber, an organic raw material that is widely available. Mabesa guaranteed that the cellulose in its products came from sustainably managed forests, suppliers respected the rights of workers and local communities, and harvests preserved ecological biodiversity. Its diapers also contained a plastic and superabsorbent cover containing both petroleum-based and natural materials.
- Reducing electricity consumption. The energy that Mabesa's manufacturing operations used was produced by the company's wind farm.
- Reducing water consumption and reusing water in irrigation systems in forested areas.

- Reducing waste and improving waste management.
- Contributing to reforestation programs in Mexico.
- Complying with environmental certification criteria. Mabesa Tijuana was certified by the Forest Stewardship Council for responsibly sourcing forest products.[2]

The company would go on to expand its sustainability efforts with its Bio Baby diapers.

Bio Baby's Origins

As the Introduction mentions, one of the main concerns about using disposable products is the waste they generate. Bio Baby was born out of the efforts of Richard Halbinger-Carmona, the company's marketing manager, to improve Mabesa's sustainability performance. Among the questions he pondered over the years before developing Bio Baby included: Were the company's efforts enough to make it sustainable? Does a company need to have a concrete sustainability plan and structure? Was Mabesa missing the opportunity to position itself as a sustainable company?[3]

Halbinger began asking these questions long before Mabesa created and marketed Bio Baby. Indeed, even before Mabesa's CEO asked him in 2005 to find a way to compete against Huggies in the premium market, Halbinger had already been thinking about an innovative product. An idea occurred to him after hearing environmentalists make the following claims:

- On average a baby will use 3,700 diapers during its life. It is estimated that a staggering 93 billion disposable diapers are used throughout the world each year.
- More than 1,500 liters of crude oil, 360 kilograms of plastic, and an enormous amount of water are needed to produce the 3,700 diapers each baby will use. Each diaper takes at least 300 years to biodegrade.[4]
- In best-case scenarios, diapers are deposited in landfills, altering the natural sediment of these places; the ones that do not reach

the landfills are dumped into rivers, ditches, and manholes or even thrown into the ocean.

- The plastic bags in which diapers are wrapped are another environmental hazard, as this plastic takes even longer to decompose and pollutes soil and water.
- More than 100 viruses can survive in feces for two weeks outside the human body. This means that many viruses from diapers end up in landfills, where they are ingested by insects and mammals and potentially passed on to humans. The viruses can also infiltrate underground water sources and contaminate rivers.

Many companies that produce disposable diapers defend their products by suggesting that cloth diapers use more water and create more pollution, through detergents that wash into rivers, lakes, and the ocean when the diapers are washed. Provoked by these claims, Halbinger began to take an interest in finding sustainable diaper options. By coincidence, he had invited a vendor from Texas-based PHOENIX Plastics for a visit in 2003. PHOENIX sells plastics to the hygiene industry, and among its products was a type of biodegradable plastic. Halbinger told the vendor about his idea to manufacture diapers with good performance and from biodegradable materials. Specifically, Halbinger wanted to know if PHOENIX could produce a plastic that would make diapers biodegradable. The vendor said it was possible.

Halbinger then hired Merc-Gfk, a prominent market research company, to perform a study to: (1) analyze the potential of the biodegradable diaper concept; (2) determine the strengths and weaknesses of the concept; (3) identify consumers' willingness to purchase this new type of diaper; (4) determine the degree of overall public acceptance of this new product; and (5) evaluate the variables that the target market would consider when deciding whether to purchase its usual diaper brand or this new product.

Merc-Gfk conducted 300 interviews with mothers who had babies up to 2.5 years old and belonged to a B/C+ socioeconomic status (see Table 11.2), among the highest living standards in Mexico.[5] These

Table 11.2 Socioeconomic levels in Mexico

Level A/B : The highest standard of living in Mexico. Individuals within this segment not only have all of their basic needs met, but also have the means to invest and plan for the future. Currently this segment represents 6.8% of urban households in the country.
Level C+: The second highest living standard in Mexico. Like the Level A/B, they too have all of their basic needs met, however their investments and savings for the future are limited. This segment represents 14.25 % of the urban households in the country.
Level C: Individuals within this segment have comfortable living conditions. They have basic entertainment and technology amenities. Currently they represent 17% of the urban household population.
Level C-: Households at this level have certain basic needs met such as housing and sanitation, and have the rudimentary equipment and services to guarantee a basic level of comfort and practicality at their homes. This segment currently represents 17.1% of urban households in Mexico.
Level D+: This segment only has the minimum infrastructure and sanitation in their homes. At the moment, they represent 18.5% of the urban households in the country.
Level D: Individuals in this segment do have housing, but they lack the majority of basic goods and services. This segment represents 21.4% of the urban households in Mexico.
Level E: The segment with the lowest quality or standard of living. They lack all basic home goods and services. They currently represent 5% of urban households in the country.

Source: Niveles Socio Económicos AMAI, "¿Cuántos Niveles Socioeconómicos hay y cuáles son sus principales características?".

interviews lasted 20 minutes and were conducted face-to-face at the mothers' homes. This study corroborated Halbinger's understanding that consumers were pleased with Kimberly-Clark's Huggies. It showed that consumers were most familiar with brands like Huggies, Pampers, and Kleen Bebé, but also that they understood concepts of eco-friendliness and had positive opinions of them (Figure 11.1).

With these results in hand, Halbinger went to the company's CEO and told him about his idea that, in Halbinger's words, "will make a great impact in the diaper market." He said, "I have found a niche that is worried about the environmental impact that diapers cause, and we can offer them a unique and innovative solution to satisfy their needs.

Phrases that you associate with the concepts of "organic", "biodegradable," and "eco-friendly"

Total Sample Size (300)

The concepts were clear for the majority of respondents. These words were automatically associated with environmental care, and reduction or lack of pollution.

ORGANIC		BIODEGRADABLE		ECO-FRIENDLY	
Recyclable	16	Recycle products	22	Does not pollute	25
Natural	13	Does not pollute	19	Cares for nature	23
Does not pollute	11	Does not harm the environment	14	Protects the environment	16
Food / Meals	9	Quickly disintegrates	12	No littering	13
Trash	6	Does not disrupt nature	8	Trees	7
Clean	6	Soap / detergent	7	Water care	7
Does not harm the environment	6	Paper	7	Hygiene	7
Can be reused	6	Reincorporates into nature	6	Does not harm plants	6
Paper	5	Falls apart or disintegrates	6	Water	6
Human Organism	4	Plastic / Plastics	4	Recyclable	5
Plants	4	Diaper	4	Plant trees	5
Peels	3	More natural	4	Plants	5
Don't know	9	Don't know	7	Natural origin	5
				Don't know	1

Q9. Tell me 3 phrases you associate with the concept of "organic"

Q10. Tell me 3 phrases you associate with the concept of "biodegradable"

Q11. Tell me 3 phrases you associate with the concept of "eco-friendly"

Figure 11.1 Phrases respondents associated with "organic," "biodegradable," and "eco-friendly."

Source: Gfk Mexico.

I have been conducting some studies that indicate that mothers would be willing to buy such a product."

The CEO liked the idea and said, "Work on it some more, consolidate it, and convince me. Remember that the main objective is to have a product that can take market share away from Huggies in the *premium* sector."[6]

Two years passed and Mabesa's situation did not improve. It wasn't gaining market share and was still unable to compete in the premium market. Meanwhile, Halbinger continued to develop his idea. At the end of 2005, he conducted an exploratory study in Mexico City to test the eco-friendly diaper concept and examine this new product's potential in an upscale market sector. This market study was conducted with mothers aged 25–35, who belonged to the highest-income socioeconomic groups (Level A/B) and who regularly used disposable diapers.

According to the mothers who were surveyed, the most important attributes of diapers were absorption capacity, snug fits, sizes for infants of different ages, Velcro waistbands, and eye-catching designs. These mothers believed that expensive diapers were higher-quality than cheaper ones. They also said they were willing to try new brands, explore different products, and give their brand loyalty to the best diapers at the best prices.

When the mothers were asked their opinion about the "ideal diaper," the majority said it must be biodegradable, since they were concerned about the pollution caused by disposable diapers. However, the women emphasized that biodegradability should not come at the expense of diapers' function. The results suggested that biodegradability could be considered a value-added differentiator for Mabesa's brand, which could increase usage as long as the diapers kept their performance and convenience. Mabesa considered all of these factors in Bio Baby's development.

The study also examined these mothers' brand perception and confirmed that the "top of mind" brand was Huggies. To them, Huggies came closest to the ideal diaper. One of the most important conclusions of the market study was that the concept of a biodegradable disposable diaper, although attractive for most respondents, was not in itself enough to determine purchasing decisions. These decisions depended on babies' comfort as well as a diaper's price. However, for baby diapers, purchase decisions were often impacted by "umbrella branding": marketing that links new products to established brands. This strong brand-based market meant that a new Mabesa product would have to differentiate itself by its new eco-friendly characteristics.

Shortly after this second study, Mabesa hired a new commercial director, who would be Halbinger's supervisor. This new director, Carlos Espinosa, came from SCA-Svenska Cellulosa Aktiebolaget, a global company based in Stockholm and dedicated to the manufacturing of absorbent, disposable hygiene products. The company's most prestigious brands in the Mexican market were Regio toilet paper, Saba women's sanitary pads, and Tena adult diapers. Halbinger presented his value-generating ideas to Espinosa, along with the new research indicating their promise. The new commercial director liked

Halbinger's proposal and together they began to refocus Mabesa's marketing efforts.

Bio Baby: Launch and Response

To come up with the concept for Bio Baby, Halbinger had identified the market's "unmet needs." He concluded that the qualitative research indicated mothers who bought premium diapers felt "green guilt" about throwing away disposable products. Mabesa focused on this market niche, designing a product with excellent performance and differentiated by "eco-friendliness."[7]

The design process resulted in the Bio Baby diaper, an eco-friendly diaper alternative that didn't sacrifice absorption, durability, or comfort. Bio Baby was the only diaper that had substituted the nonrenewable external band and absorbent materials for more sustainable ones. It was estimated that eight out of ten mothers would be willing to switch to Bio Baby over the premium brands they regularly purchased. Bio Baby was launched in the Mexican market in 2007, positioned in the premium sector.

A week after its launch, Kimberly-Clark began a smear campaign against the brand, arguing that it was impossible to produce a 100 percent biodegradable product. Kimberly-Clark spent two months and US$5 million, almost the entirety of its annual Mexican advertising budget, on this effort.

Mabesa designed a strategy to defend itself. The company had never claimed Bio Baby was 100 percent biodegradable. Its advertising had always indicated that Bio Baby had some biodegradable and eco-friendly traits. Because Mabesa did not have the same advertising budget as Kimberly-Clark, the company needed to get its message out in ways that maximized its reach without exceeding its budget. Mabesa hired Avatar, an Argentinian advertising agency that had defended a local bottling company against a larger competitor's claim that its bottled water caused cancer. For Mabesa's campaign, Avatar proposed making use of social networks. Even though social media was not used as widely in 2007 as it is today, it was already used by Bio

Baby's target market. Those who bought premium brands preferred the internet to traditional venues like TV, radio, or print journalism. The company created a "Blog for Bio Baby" that exposed what it considered to be unfair attacks by Kimberly-Clark, and emphasized the benefits of Bio Baby for the environment, babies' health, and families' budgets.

The campaign was a success. Mabesa achieved its Bio Baby target objective, which was to have a 1 percent share of the Mexican premium market within its first year. At the end of 2007, it reached a 1.2 percent market share, which increased to 1.3 percent in 2010. By 2013, Bio Baby had reached 1.5 percent market penetration, having become profitable that year, and began to win market share from Huggies in large Mexican cities.

Bio Baby's price was slightly lower than Huggies, but the brand was not as profitable, as some of the material used to make the diapers was more expensive. In 2015, Bio Baby reached a 2.1 percent market share in the Mexican premium market. At this point, Halbinger wondered: Were there other strategies related to sustainability that could capture consumers' interest?

International Strategy

Bio Baby's story unfolded beyond just Mexico, though. Before launching Bio Baby, Mabesa's financial estimations confirmed that domestic sales alone would not be enough to sustain the brand. Therefore, the company eyed a larger market for its eco-friendly product line. In 2006, Walmart USA announced it would give preference to providers offering sustainable products. The research and development manager of Valor Brands, an American company that sold Mabesa products under different private labels, contacted Halbinger to tell him about the opportunity to enter the US market via Bio Baby. Five months later, Valor Brands introduced the disposable diaper in the United States. Among its new retailers was Walmart USA. Before long 80 percent of Mabesa's sales in the United States, via Valor Brands, were eco-friendly.

As of 2015, Bio Baby was the only product of its kind in Latin America, with eco-friendly materials that could help reduce the environmental impact of disposable diapers. It contained a large number of sustainable and biodegradable materials that could decompose safely and more quickly than conventional diapers. In the domestic sector, Bio Baby reached wealthier households through a growing niche market concerned about sustainability. (The Bio Baby product line also included Bio Baby wet wipes and training pants.) However, because of the need for additional revenue, Mabesa's success with Bio Baby depended on achieving the same niche in the United States, the world's largest market for diapers.

Because Bio Baby was costlier for the company to produce, consumers pay about 15 percent more for them than mid-sector disposable diapers from Ontex (the company has continued to sell Bio Baby after its acquisition of Mabesa). Consumers, however, can see that Bio Baby's sustainability justifies the higher price. At present, Bio Baby is marketed in Mexico, Spain, Central America, Portugal, France, England, China, Korea, United Arab Emirates, Saudi Arabia, and Dubai. It is also sold under private label brands in the United States, Canada, and parts of Europe and Asia.

Bio Baby found its place in the market as a pioneer disposable diaper with biodegradable materials, and it is now the best-selling eco-friendly product in Mexico. Worldwide, only four companies are manufacturing disposable diapers with any environmentally friendly characteristics: two in Europe, one in Australia, and Ontex, the Mexican market leader. As the demand for healthy lifestyles and eco-friendly products grows, Ontex is confident that Bio Baby diapers will continue to be a viable alternative for a growing number of eco-conscious consumers. The company hopes to build on the product's success and has a goal of launching a 100 percent sustainable disposable diaper by 2020.

Conclusion

This case study is a clear example of how companies, even in polluting industries, can find products that allow them to become more profitable while also reducing their environmental footprints. Mabesa did both by developing an innovative disposable diaper that had a smaller impact on the environment than competitors' products without sacrificing quality or performance. Although this diaper was targeted at the premium market, it was not inaccessible to other segments as it was not the most expensive diaper option available.

Although Mabesa and now Ontex's sustainability strategy offers lessons for other companies, Bio Baby itself would be hard to replicate. Mabesa developed a blend of natural materials that replaced polluting ones and were not hazardous to users' health. These innovations were protected by patents, an example of how developing a sustainable product further added to Bio Baby's competitive advantage. Mabesa also produced all of the energy consumed by the company at its wind farm. Aside from being a more sustainable practice that distinguished Mabesa from its competitors, renewable energy reduced costs for the company.

In addition to its eco-friendly products and renewable energy use, Mabesa achieved other goals it laid out in its sustainable business strategy. It participated in monarch butterfly sanctuary efforts in Mexico and donated to several nongovernmental organizations, including Reforestemos México and the World Wildlife Fund. Although the company is making progress in its sustainability efforts, Mabesa still has a long way to go as Ontex in Mexico. It has struggled to define and strengthen its sustainability strategy. Additional environmentally conscious practices need to be initiated by top management, so that they will infiltrate and flow into the organization more easily. The CSR team believes that manufacturing a completely sustainable disposable diaper is not enough; among other things, the company must reduce pollution and have sustainable thinking permeate all stakeholders (employees, suppliers, and customers), in order to become a truly sustainable company.

Chapter 12

WATER USE EFFICIENCY INITIATIVES IN NESTLÉ'S VALUE CHAIN AND THE IMPLICATIONS OF THE COMPANY'S BUSINESS MODEL

Hellen Quinonez

Abstract

Water scarcity is one of today's most pressing global environmental issues, and global water demand is expected to increase by more than half by mid-century. Some multinational corporations are reducing their water footprint, and are discovering that such steps also improve their business model. Nestlé, the world's largest food and beverage corporation, has been widely criticized in the past for environmental and public health failings, but it has begun to address its lapses with its Creating Shared Value sustainability strategy. This case study focuses on the water-use sustainability strategies adopted by Nestlé in Mexico, specifically its Zero-Water powdered milk plant and the efforts of its milk suppliers. It describes the creation of the Zero-Water plant at Nestlé Mexico, and explains the philosophy behind the Creating Shared Value campaign. With a reduction in water consumption from 2,000 cubic meters per day down to zero, the Zero-Water plant provides a model for other multinational corporations to decrease their water use.

Introduction

Founded in 1866 in Switzerland, Nestlé is now the largest food and beverage business in the world, with operations in 150 countries. In

1867, its founder, Henri Nestlé, became concerned about infant mortality rates, and developed a lactic powder for children who could not be breastfed by their mothers. The subsequent research and development for healthy foods based on science has become the core business of this multinational company.

As of 2015, Nestlé had over 300,000 employees worldwide, 436 factories, total global sales equivalent to US$88.5 billion per year, and a yearly net profit of US$9 billion. The company produces and distributes products under various name brands worldwide, including baby foods (Cerelac, Gerber); bottled water (Nestlé Pure Life, Perrier); cereals (Cini Minis, Fitness, Nesquik); candy (Nestlé Crunch, Kit Kat); coffee (Nescafé, Dolce Gusto, Coffee-Mate); frozen food (Maggi, DiGiorno); dairy products (Carnation, Nido); drinks (Nestea, Milo); prepared foods (CHEF, Lean Cuisine); nutrition (Boost, Peptamen); ice cream (Dreyer's, Häagen-Dazs); petcare (Beneful); and weight management products (Optifast). All of these products require water to produce.

Nestlé's newfound leadership role in sustainability is remarkable, given its history of controversy involving baby formula and groundwater depletion. The company's aggressive marketing of its baby formula since the 1970s has led to a long-running international boycott of its products by organizations that claim the use of milk substitute creates health risks for infants. Nestlé has also been accused of depleting aquifers in Canada and the United States for use in its bottled water products.

Nestlé now aligns its corporate principles with the United Nations Global Compact, which calls for companies to advance human rights, labor, environmental, and anticorruption goals. It is one of nearly 8,000 companies in 170 countries that have signed on to this agreement. Nestlé also has partnerships with the United Nations Development Program and the United Nations Global Compact's CEO Water Mandate. This mandate, also known as Corporate Water Disclosure, requires multinational companies to keep all stakeholders updated on their water management practices and inform them of any strategic responses to problems that arise.[1]

Nestlé's Best Practices

Within the company, Nestlé has initiated a sustainability strategy called Creating Shared Value (CSV), which has allowed it to achieve several sustainability goals worldwide. Among these goals are collaborating with 760,000 farmers who supply the company and reducing cumulative direct water withdrawals per metric ton of product by 41.2 percent between 2005 and 2015.[2]

Nestlé's value chain is formed by agriculture, suppliers, Nestlé factories, retail channels, and consumers. Agriculture is by far the largest user of water in the world. According to the United Nations, it accounts for 70 percent of global water withdrawals. Climate change, human population growth, and inefficient use are among the most major agricultural water issues. According to Hashimoto, water problems could have severe consequences for agriculture: "Increasing variability in precipitation could endanger species and crops and lead to a decline in food production."[3]

In 2015, the International Water Management Institute (IWMI) reported an increase of 12 percent in the world's cultivated area over the past 50 years, and a doubling of irrigated area—from 343 million to 744 million acres.[4] Two liters of water per day are enough for direct human consumption, but 3,000 liters are required to produce one person's daily food supply. Globally, 43 percent of agricultural water comes from groundwater. According to Tilman et al., "forty per cent of crop production comes from the 16% of agricultural land that is irrigated" and "unless water-use efficiency is increased, greater agricultural production will require increased irrigation."[5] The IWMI concludes that "the question that has to be addressed is whether we can sustainably extend and intensify agricultural production"[6] in large part because of water scarcity. Diminishing water supply and quality, a growing population and intensifying agricultural systems require corporations to make their value chains more sustainable. Water scarcity is becoming a risk and a limitation for growth in the food industry and for Nestlé. The risks are physical (water stress, scarcity, declining quality), financial (higher water prices, rising discharge costs), and social (regulatory limits on withdrawals and loss of social license to operate).[7]

Nestlé's Sustainable Water Use Strategy

Nestlé began operations in Mexico in 1930 and today has 3 regulating centers, 28 sales offices, 12 plants (with another under construction), 8 distribution centers, a center for research and development, and a central office, located in Mexico City. Nestlé operates in Mexico in the context of the country's acute water challenges. In 2013, the country had a 0.41 water stress index, considered moderate to critical by CONAGUA, the Mexican federal water commission. CONAGUA calculates its water stress index by dividing the amount of rainfall by the quantity of water extracted. López-Morales argues that "one in every six of Mexican aquifers are in overdraft, and the quantity and quality of surface water is being compromised with diversion infrastructure, lack of wastewater treatment, and mismanagement, which also negatively affects the provision of essential services from the country's ecosystems."[8]

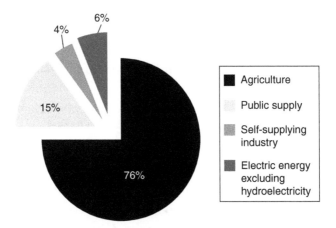

Figure 12.1 Volume distribution concessioned by consumptive use.
Source: CONAGUA.

According to CONAGUA's *Numeragua 2014* report on water usage statistics, of every 100 liters of water used, 76 liters are employed in agriculture (Figure 12.1), with 50 liters extracted from surface water and 25 liters from the subsoil. Seventy-four million acres of Mexican land are devoted to agriculture, and 18 percent of that land is watered by some form of irrigation—the rest is rain-fed.[9] The *Numeragua* report also states that Mexican agriculture uses 900 liters of water per kilogram of corn, 3,400 liters per kilogram of rice, and 15,500 per kilogram of beef. Nestlé is a large purchaser of raw agricultural materials and ingredients. The crops the company purchases consume 63.5 billion cubic meters of water, making sustainable practices an important pillar of social responsibility for the company.

This concern about water use is especially important since currently, 36.7 percent of Nestlé's factories around the world are located in water-stressed regions. Nestlé requires water to wash raw materials, reconstitute dried ingredients, cook products, clean equipment, and provide sanitation services for employees. The company withdrew a total of 140 million cubic meters of water in 2015 at 485 factories. To assess water availability risks at every operating site, it employs the Nestlé Combined Water Stress Index.[10]

In Mexico, Nestlé has addressed water availability and scarcity with several projects related to water along its value chain. Among these are a rural development project involving a collaboration between local farmers and Nestlé's Zero-Water powdered milk plant in Lagos de Moreno, a city of more than 150,000 residents in the central Mexican state of Jalisco. The water use patterns in Lagos de Moreno and Jalisco are similar to those presented above for Mexico more broadly. Agriculture is, by far, the largest consumer of water in Jalisco. According to Jalisco's State Water Commission (CEA for its acronym in Spanish), 97 percent of surface water and 83.67 percent of underground water are destined for agricultural activities in Lagos de Moreno and the surrounding area. Because of such extensive water use, Nestlé works closely with the region's dairy farmers who supply the Lagos de Moreno plant with milk. This not only ensures a good quality product but it also offers Nestlé an opportunity to train the milk producers in best water use practices and promote water sustainability.

View from the Field

Rogelio Aguirre, the sustainability director for Nestlé in Lagos de Moreno, took me on a visit to two medium-sized milk suppliers in

2016. These farmers told me that the information Nestlé provides has allowed them to save water and energy. Likewise, Nestlé offered financing that allowed these farmers to buy state-of-the-art irrigation equipment, implement efficient irrigation systems, install bio-digesters to break organic material down into fertilizer, and educate themselves about how to recollect water and reuse it in its operations.

The first milk supplier we visited owns 95 cows that he said produce a total 4,000 liters of milk per day. His original operation produced only about half as much milk per cow, and he attributes this increase in production to several Nestlé technician recommendations: "drip irrigation, low use of fertilizers and use of manure in the corn production which increases the quality of the forage to feed the cows." He also believes that "continuous innovation is what keeps my milk production in the market." He explained, "I have reduced the water consumption by 30 percent and increased the production of forage by 50 percent."

According to this same producer, the biggest challenges of producing sustainable milk are his workers' resistance to change and the high initial cost of implementing new and sustainable practices. But the benefits of sustainable practices outweigh the difficulties, he argued. "I stop consuming water and it stays there for the future generations," he said. "There is support from government and other organizations [like Nestlé] to implement sustainable strategies."

The second milk supplier produces around 2,000 liters of milk per day. When he implemented sprinkler irrigation with second-hand equipment, he was able to reduce his water consumption by 30–40 percent. The main challenges he mentioned are "milk prices, an increase in the cost of inputs, and diseases." He is satisfied with the advice Nestlé has provided and cited the advantages of "projects to bring the water to the stables, solar panels, dams to conserve the water, the use of a bio-digester to save electricity." The benefit for the community, he added, is the adoption of the same sustainable practices by his neighbors.

By 2015, Nestlé had trained 738 milk producers in Mexico on topics like water use efficiency and the use of renewable energy. Aguirre told me that "the suppliers are obliged to adopt Nestlé's best practices and we assess them through a platform called Response-Inducing Sustainability Evaluation (RISE) where we evaluate ten indicators: animal production, water use and energy consumption, crop production, work conditions, and other issues."

Sustainability Analysis: Nestlé's Zero-Water Plant

Above and beyond Nestlé's work with local farmers, the company's Zero-Water powdered milk plant in Lagos de Moreno has been its major technological advancement related to water in the region. Before the Zero-Water plant was built, this factory consumed 2,000 cubic meters of water per day. After the factory built the zero water facilities and was fully operational, that total was reduced to zero. In its report *Nestlé in Society*, the company describes its Zero-Water plant in Lagos de Moreno.[11] Instead of using groundwater, the factory captures the water that would typically be lost through evaporation in the process of making powdered milk.

In an interview conducted inside the Nestlé factory in Lagos de Moreno, Nuria Navarrete, Nestlé's water resources coordinator, and plant engineer Carlos Gutiérrez explained that Nestlé modified the factory between 2011 and 2014. The first phase, which implemented various water-saving measures, allowed the factory to cut its water consumption by 22 percent. In the second phase, the factory converted its "cow-water" (the water that is left after dehydrating milk) into potable water. Through this final phase, the factory began to operate without any groundwater withdrawal.

Nuria Navarrete explained that the factory is located in a water-stressed part of Mexico, but in 2012 Nestlé considered it a high water consumption factory. "On average, the quantity of milk that arrives every day is 1.4 million liters. Lagos de Moreno is the factory that receives more milk because it has national and export powdered milk production," she said. Other Nestlé Mexico plants receive less milk, and "the milk that is collected is taken to a concentration center and goes through a process of ultrafiltration and nanofiltration to reduce the quantity of water in order to concentrate it. The water that is removed is used to clean these centers."

The biggest challenges for implementing the Zero-Water project were the large initial investment, staff training, and knowledge acquisition it required, according to Gutierrez. "The main objective of this factory was not to stop consuming water, but to consume water in a different and sustainable way," he said. "Due to the increasing prices of water due to scarcity in the region we had to implement new and better ways to use the water."

To undertake projects like the Zero-Water plant, Nestlé has had to make sustainability a financial priority. According to Nuria Navarrete, 18–20 percent of Nestlé's total global investment budget is authorized for water and energy projects. Francis Pérez, Nestlé Mexico's director of CSV, said that in the past five years, Nestlé has invested more than US$49 million in environmental initiatives across the world, including over US$7 million in the Zero-Water plant. In another interview, Francis Pérez explained the decision-making process behind the Zero-Water plant: "Instead of generating a savings it increased the operations cost by 10 million pesos per year. Despite this, we went ahead with it. To financially evaluate the projects that have to do with sustainability what we do is to analyze the business opportunity in the future with respect to the value of this resource."

Nestlé Joins a Growing Global Chorus

Nestlé is not just taking steps outlined above in Mexico out of responsible stewardship of natural resources. As Daniel C. Esty and Andrew S. Winston explain, "Companies that manage nature's bounty and boundaries best will minimize vulnerabilities and move ahead of their competitors."[12] Other companies have also discovered the competitive advantage of sustainable water use.

According to Alabau et al., "Given the challenges and opportunities associated with water stress, many companies are beginning to design programs to manage water use in their direct operations."[13] The authors mention initiatives some companies have undertaken to use water more efficiently. For example, because Coca-Cola in India faced many political and legal complications due to its excessive use of groundwater, the company developed a new water stewardship goal: "By 2020, safely return to communities and nature an amount of water equal to what we use in our finished beverages and their production." By 2013, Coca-Cola had achieved 68 percent replenishment. Alabau et al. also describe Unilever's "Sustainable Living Plan" to help consumers use water more effectively, improve factory water efficiency, and use water strategically in agriculture. And finally, they mention Colgate-Palmolive's Sustainability Plan, including its Making Every Drop of Water Count Program focused on water stewardship.

Nestlé has now become a multinational corporate leader in water stewardship. In *Nestlé in Society*, the company states that "water is critical to Nestlé's business and their value chain, yet global withdrawals are predicted to exceed supply by 40% by 2030."[14] The company says it strives to use water efficiently and steward it responsibly in the water bodies from which it harvests resources for its products. Nestlé's report also argues that its "food and beverages facilities, and particularly [its] water bottling plants, naturally attract attention for the water they withdraw. And when these plants are situated in locations experiencing water stress or drought, that stakeholder attention only heightens."

The foundation for Nestlé's sustainability actions and CSV are the company's corporate principles: nutrition, health and well-being; quality assurance and product safety; consumer communication; human rights in its business activities; leadership and personal responsibility; safety and health at work; supplier and customer relations; environmental sustainability; agriculture and rural development; and water.

In its *Creating Shared Value* report, Nestlé lists what it considers its biggest global water use achievements.[15] Notably, it has saved 1.7 million cubic meters of water through 362 water-saving projects. All Nestlé's sustainability strategies are considered both long-term investments for the company and benefits for the community. This CSV long-term perspective allows Nestlé to protect its business operations, deliver sustainable products to society, and preserve the environment for future generations.

Conclusion

Nestlé's strategies for sustainable water consumption are important not only for the company, but for all stakeholders involved. By taking action on water scarcity and its consequences for future generations, Nestlé spreads awareness to the community and other companies.

Concrete action toward ensuring water availability to future generations is part of the company's sustainability strategy. However, the strategy is also important for securing the continuity of the business. By safeguarding the supply of one of its most important inputs, Nestlé is assuring that in the long run it will have the resource at hand. As Esty and Winston have argued, "Companies that successfully manage environmental risks lower their operating costs, reduce the cost of capital, drive up stock market valuations, and keep insurance premiums reasonable. They also avoid the indirect costs of business interruption and lost good will."[16] Through active management of its upstream supply, Nestlé has ensured consistent resource management starting at the beginning of its value chain.

In Mexico, it is clear that Nestlé's objectives and its CSV approach are being accomplished in the best way possible. Despite the large investment made in its Zero-Water plant, Nestlé has ensured a continuous supply of its most important input, which it calls its most important "asset"—water. The Zero-Water factory is the largest investment that Nestlé has made in sustainability projects in Mexico and it will ensure its operations continue in the Lagos de Moreno region due to the dependence on this valuable resource during scarcity periods. This demand for water suggests that Nestlé's sustainability efforts are likely to pay off substantially in the future. Nestlé saw water risk on the horizon and acted before the company's water consumption became a drain on its finances and a burden for Mexican society.

NOTES

INTRODUCTION

1 Johan Rockström and Mattias Klum, *Big World, Small Planet: Abundance within Planetary Boundaries* (New Haven, CT: Yale University Press, 2015).

2 C. Anne Claus et al., "Disaster, Degradation, Dystopia," in *The International Handbook of Political Ecology*, edited by Raymond L. Bryant (Cheltenham, UK: Edward Elgar Publishing, 2017), 291–304.

3 Peter Bakker, "A New Corporate Performance Measurement Framework Can Encourage Sustainable Success, For Business and For Society," *We Mean Business*, June 24, 2016, https://www.wemeanbusinesscoalition.org/blog/a-new-corporate-performance-measurement-framework-can-encourage-sustainable-success-for-business-and-for-society/.

4 David A. Lubin and Daniel C. Esty, "The Sustainability Imperative," *Harvard Business Review* 88, no. 5 (2010): 42–50.

5 Alan Murray and Geoffrey Smith, "CEO Daily: Tuesday, 6th June," *Fortune CEO Daily* (web log), June 6, 2017, http://fortune.com/2017/06/06/ceo-daily-tuesday-6th-june/.

6 Daniel C. Esty, "Bottom-Up Climate Fix," *New York Times*, September 21, 2014, A:25 sec.

7 United Nations, United Nations Framework Convention on Climate Change, *The Paris Agreement*, December 12, 2015, Article 6.

8 United Nations, United Nations General Assembly, *The Future We Want*, September 11, 2012.

9 GRI, United Nations Global Compact, and WBCSD, *SDG Compass Guide: The Guide for Business Action on the SDGs*, 2015.

10 Hank Boerner, "The Results Are In: Sustainable, Responsible, Impact Investing by U.S. Asset Managers At All-Time High—$8 Trillion!," *Governance and Accountability Institute Sustainability Update*, November 16, 2016, http://ga-institute.com/Sustainability-Update/2016/11/16/the-results-are-in-sustainable-responsible-impact-investing-by-u-s-asset-managers-at-all-time-high-8-trillion/.

11 Daniel C. Esty and Todd Cort, "Corporate Sustainability Metrics: What Investors Need and Don't Get," *Journal of Environmental Investing* 8, no. 1 (2017): 11–53.

12 David A. Lubin and Daniel C. Esty, "Bridging the Sustainability Gap," *MIT Sloan Management Review* 55, no. 4 (2014): 18–21.

13 Sustainalytics, *Inversión Responsable y Sostenible: Visión General, Prácticas Actuales y Tendencia*, July 2014.

14 Esty and Cort, "Corporate Sustainability Metrics: What Investors Need and Don't Get," 11–53.

15 Jack Ewing and Neal E. Boudette, "As VW Pleads Guilty in U.S. Over Diesel Scandal, Trouble Looms in Europe," *New York Times*, March 10, 2017, B:1 sec.

16 Stash, "VW Scandal: How Has It Impacted Volkswagen's Stock?," *Investopedia*, October 5, 2016, https://www.investopedia.com/news/vw-scandal-how-has-it-impacted-volkswagens-stock-vlkay/.

17 Daniel C. Esty and Andrew S. Winston, *Green to Gold: How Smart Companies Use Environmental Strategy to Innovate, Create Value, and Build Competitive Advantage* (New Haven, CT: Yale University Press, 2006), 129–30.

18 Jatinder J. Singh, Oriol Iglesias, and Joan Manel Batista-Foguet, "Does Having an Ethical Brand Matter? The Influence of Consumer Perceived Ethicality on Trust, Affect and Loyalty," *Journal of Business Ethics* 111, no. 4 (2012): 541–49.

19 Daniel Servitje Montull, interview by Daniel Esty in Mexico City, April 27, 2015.

20 Liz Maw, "What Workers Want Is What the World Needs," *Stanford Social Innovation Review*, May, 24, 2012, https://ssir.org/articles/entry/what_workers_want_is_what_the_world_needs.

21 Esty and Winston, *Green to Gold*. See also Daniel C. Esty and P. J. Simmons, *The Green to Gold Business Playbook: How to Implement Sustainability Practices for Bottom-Line Results in Every Business Function* (Hoboken, NJ: Wiley, 2011).

22 Unilever, "Unilever to Acquire Quala Personal Care and Homecare Brands," *Unilever*, May 15, 2017, https://www.unilever.com/news/Press-releases/2017/unilever-to-acquire-quala-personal-care-and-homecare-brands.html.

Chapter 1:   WATER CONSERVATION IN SCARCITY CONDITIONS: CORPORATE SUSTAINABILITY AT MEXICO'S FEMSA GROUP

1 FEMSA, *Annual Report 2015*, March 9, 2016.

2 Max E. Clarkson, "A Stakeholder Framework for Analyzing and Evaluating Corporate Social Performance," *Academy of Management Review* 20, no. 1 (1995): 92–117.

3 Amy J. Hillman and Gerald D. Keim, "Shareholder Value, Stakeholder Management, and Social Issues: What's the Bottom Line?," *Strategic Management Journal* 22, no. 2 (2001): 125–39.

4 John L. Campbell, "Why Would Corporations Behave in Socially Responsible Ways? An Institutional Theory of Corporate Social Responsibility," *Academy of Management Review* 32, no. 3 (2007): 946–67.

5 FEMSA, "Who We Are," http://www.femsa.com/en/meet-femsa/our-beginning/who-we-are.

6 David A. Lubin and Daniel C. Esty, "The Sustainability Imperative," *Harvard Business Review* 88, no. 5 (2010): 45.

7 FEMSA Sustainability, *Annual Report*, 2013, http://www.sustainabilityreport.femsa.com/2013/pdf/gri_2013.pdf.

8 José de Jesús Návar Cháidez, "Water Scarcity and Degradation in the Rio San Juan Watershed of Northeastern Mexico," *Frontera Norte* 23, no. 46 (2011): 125–50.

9 FEMSA, " 'Regios' Unite in Favor of Nature," *FEMSA*, September 18, 2013, http://www.femsa.com/en/femsa-news/regios-unite-favor-nature/.

Chapter 2: WALMART MEXICO: CLEAN ENERGY TO REDUCE COSTS AND IMPROVE CORPORATE IMAGE

1 Daniel C. Esty and Andrew S. Winston, *Green to Gold: How Smart Companies Use Environmental Strategy to Innovate, Create Value, and Build Competitive Advantage* (New Haven, CT: Yale University Press, 2006), 7–8.

2 Emma M. Lloyd, " 'Greening' the Supply Chain: Why Corporate Leaders Make It Matter," *Journal of Land Use & Environmental Law* 27, no. 1 (2011): 31–68.

3 David Barstow, "Vast Mexico Bribery Case Hushed up by Wal-Mart after Top-Level Struggle," *New York Times*, April 21, 2012, http://www.nytimes.com/2012/04/22/business/at-wal-mart-in-mexico-a-bribe-inquiry-silenced.html?pagewanted=all&_r=0.

4 Esty and Winston, *Green to Gold*.

5 Manuel Gómez Peña, former director of sustainability, Walmart Mexico, interview conducted for the case study "Walmart de Mexico: Investing in Renewable Energy," Global Network Case 101–11, Yale University, http://nexus.som.yale.edu/walmex.

6 Walmart, "Medio Ambiente," *Walmart de México y Centroamérica*, 2012, https://www.walmartmexico.com/responsabilidad-corporativa/medio-ambiente.

7 Gómez Peña, interview conducted for the case study "Walmart de Mexico: Investing in Renewable Energy."

Chapter 3: GRUPO VANGUARDIA REVITALIZES PLASTICS RECYCLING IN HONDURAS

1 Initially, Grupo Vanguardia's corporate social responsibility pillars included: vision, mission, and ethics; sales and responsible marketing; environmental responsibility; commitment to community; and quality of life in the company.

2 Alex Osterwalder and Yves Pigneur, *Business Model Generation: A Handbook for Visionaries, Game Changers, and Challengers* (New York, NY: John Wiley and Sons, 2010).

3 Forest Reinhardt and Richard H. K. Vietor, *Business Management and the Natural Environment* (Cincinnati, OH: South-Western College Publishing, 1996).

4 John Elkington, "Toward the Sustainable Corporation: Win-Win-Win Business Strategies for Sustainable Development," *California Management Review* 36, no. 2 (1994): 90–100.

5 Michael E. Porter and Mark R. Kramer, "Strategy and Society: The Link between Competitive Advantage and Corporate Social Responsibility," *Harvard Business Review* 84, no. 12 (December 2006): 78–92.

Chapter 4: NISSAN MEXICANA'S RENEWABLE POWER PARTNERSHIP

1 Niki Rosinski, "The Impact of Carbon Constraints on Competitiveness and Value Creation in the Automotive Industry," in *Sustainability Accounting and Reporting*, edited by S. Schaltegger, M. Bennett and R. Burritt (Springer Netherlands, 2006), 207–29.

2 Nissan, "Sustainability Report 2012," https://www.nissan-global.com/EN/DOCUMENT/PDF/SR/2012/SR12_E_All.pdf?.

3 Andre Martinuzzi, Robert Kudlak, Claus Faber, and Andre Wiman, "CSR Activities and Impacts of the Automotive Sector," Research Institute for Managing Sustainability (RIMAS), Vienna University of Economics and Business, Franz Klein Gasse 1-1190, 2011, http://www.sustainability.eu/pdf/csr/impact/IMPACT_Sector_Profile_AUTOMOTIVE.pdf.

4 Breno Nunes and David Bennett, "Green Operations Initiatives in the Automotive Industry: An Environmental Reports Analysis and Benchmarking Study," *Benchmarking: An International Journal* 17, no. 3 (2010): 396–420.

5 Martinuzzi et al., "CSR Activities and Impacts of the Automotive Sector."

6 ProMexico, *La Industria Automotriz Mexicana: Situación Actual, Retos, y Oportunidades*, 2016, http://www.promexico.mx/documentos/biblioteca/industria-automotriz-mexicana.pdf.

7 The "Sociedad Anonima de Capital Variable" (S.A. de C.V.) is translated, literally, as an anonymous society of variable capital. It is the equivalent to a US corporation in which there are stockholders.

8 Nissan, "Sustainability Report 2015," https://www.nissan-global.com/EN/ DOCUMENT/PDF/SR/2015/SR15_E_All.pdf.

9 Nissan, "Annual Report 2013," https://www.nissan-global.com/EN/ DOCUMENT/PDF/AR/2013/AR2013_E_All.pdf.

10 Nissan, "Sustainability Report 2014," https://www.nissan-global.com/EN/ DOCUMENT/PDF/SR/2014/SR14_E_All.pdf.

11 Nissan, "Sustainability Report 2015," https://www.nissan-global.com/EN/ DOCUMENT/PDF/SR/2015/SR15_E_All.pdf.

12 Ibid.

13 International Energy Agency, *Energy and Climate Change, World Energy Outlook Special Report*, 2015, https://www.iea.org/publications/freepublications/publication/WEO2015SpecialReportonEnergyandClimateChange.pdf.

14 Secretaria de Energia, *Prospectiva del Sector Eléctrico 2014–2028*, 2014, http://www.gob.mx/cms/uploads/attachment/file/351/Prospectiva-Electricidad-2014.pdf.

15 Wojciech M. Budzianowski and Dominika A. Budzianowska, "Economic Analysis of Biomethane and Electricity Generation from Biogas Using Different Support Schemes and Plant Configurations," *Energy* 88 (2015): 658–66.

16 http://nissannews.com/es-MX/nissan/mexico/releases/el-ayuntamiento-de-aguascalientes-ener-g-y-nissan-inauguran-la-generaci-n-de-energ-a-el-ctrica-limpia-a-partir-de-biog-s-en-el-relleno-sanitario-san-nicol-s.

Chapter 5:   TECNOSOL FOLLOWS THE SUN

1 Vladimir Delagneau, interview by Martha Sofia Cifuentes and Felipe Perez, 2012.

2 The size of a photovoltaic (PV) system is given by the Watt peak (Wp). This is the maximum output of a PV panel under standard conditions: ambient temperature of 25° C and 1,000 Watt/m² of irradiance.

3 FENERCA was an initiative sponsored by the United States Agency for International Development (USAID), which sought to increase the use of renewable energy in five countries in Central America (El Salvador, Guatemala, Honduras, Nicaragua, Panama). The primary objective of this initiative was to encourage the creation and development of renewable energy businesses and projects, as well as increase the participation of financial institutions in the region's energy sector. The program began in April 2000.

4 CASEIF II is a venture capital fund for Central American companies in their growth stage. The management company of CASEIF II is LAFISE Investment Management (LIM), part of the LAFISE group, a regional financial conglomerate that offers customers a complete portfolio of financial services in Central America, the Dominican Republic, Panama, Mexico, and Venezuela.

This fund invests in shares or in other quasi-equity instruments and remains a shareholder for a period of four to seven years.

5 Alex Osterwalder and Yves Pigneur, *Business Model Generation: A Handbook for Visionaries, Game Changers, and Challengers* (New York, NY: John Wiley and Sons, 2010).

6 Vijay Govindarajan and Ravi Ramamurti, "Reverse Innovation, Emerging Markets, and Global Strategy," *Global Strategy Journal* 1, no. 3–4 (2011): 191–205.

7 Forest Reinhardt and Richard Vietor, *Business Management and the Natural Environment* (Cincinnati, OH: South-Western College Publishing, 1996).

8 John Elkington, "Toward the Sustainable Corporation: Win-Win-Win Business Strategies for Sustainable Development," *California Management Review* 36, no. 2 (1994): 90–100.

9 Considering that on average each solar home system (SHS) replaced 270 liters of annual kerosene consumption at a cost of US $ 1.27 per liter, the approximate savings is US $ 342.90. If we add the cost of candles and matches, the savings would be even greater. These savings benefit families tremendously, as Tecnosol's target market of low-income rural Nicaraguans have an annual income less than US $ 1,500.

10 It is estimated that each SHS replaces approximately 270 liters per year of kerosene, which prevents the emission of 0.67 tons per year of carbon dioxide.

Chapter 6:   RIZEK PUSHES THE DOMINICAN REPUBLIC COCOA INDUSTRY TOWARD SUSTAINABILITY

1 Statistics data sets of the Agriculture Sector of the Dominican Republic, Ministry of Agriculture of the Dominican Republic.

2 Ministry of Agriculture of the Dominican Republic, "República Dominicana exporta en cacao 214 millones de dólares," 2014, http://www.agricultura. gob.do/index.php/noticias/item/511-republica-dominicana-exporta-en-cacao-214-millones-de-dolares/.

3 Amanda Berlan and Ame Bergés, "Cocoa Production in the Dominican Republic: Sustainability, Challenges and Opportunities," *Commissioned by Green & Black's*, 2013.

4 Massimiliano Wax, vice-president of Strategy and Business Development at Rizek Cacao, quoted in "*Moving up the value chain*," *FIRST Magazine*, 2016, http://www.firstmagazine.com/DownloadSpecialReportDetail.13556.ashx.

5 Center for the Promotion of Exports and Investments of the Dominican Republic, "Commercial Behavior of Organic Cacao," http://www.cei-rd.gov. do/estudios_economicos/estudios_productos/perfiles/cacao_organico.pdf.

Chapter 7: CENTROSUR LEADS THE WAY TO SUSTAINABILITY IN ECUADOR

1 Empresa Eléctrica Centro Sur C.A., "Corporate Social Responsibility Report," 2015, http://www.centrosur.gob.ec/?q=node/428.
2 Ibid.
3 Luis Urdiales, "PV Project Implementation in Taisha," thesis, University of Cuenca.
4 Ibid.
5 AGN, "En 2016 operarán 8 nuevos proyectos hidroeléctricos," *El Mercurio*, February 10, 2014, https://web.archive.org/web/20170513105023/http://www.elmercurio.com.ec:80/417607-en-2016-operaran-8-nuevos-proyectos-hidroelectricos/.
6 Juan Vasquez (engineer, Environment Department, Empresa Eléctrica Centro Sur C.A).
7 Juan Vasquez, "Gestion Integral de Materiales, Equipos y Desechos Generados en la Empresa Eléctrica Centro Sur C.A.," Department of Environment.

Chapter 8: A RESILIENT WORLD: BAVARIA BUILDS ITS CASE ON WATER

1 Steve Goldstein and William Spain, "SABMiller to Buy Bavaria for $7.8B," July 19, 2005, https://www.marketwatch.com/story/sabmiller-to-buy-colombias-bavaria-for- 78-billion.
2 Statista, "Beer production worldwide from 1998 to 2017," http://www.statista.com/statistics/270275/worldwide-beer-production/.
3 Figures vary by source. The Kirin Holding Company report for 2014 states production and consumption of 1.91 and 1.89 billion hl, respectively.
4 Figure converted from Colombian pesos (COP) to US dollars (USD) by using a foreign exchange rate of 3.058.8 COP per USD. Official information retrieved from the Banco de la Republica, March 24, 2016, http://www.banrep.gov.co/es/trm.
5 Gabriel Olivares, "Los colombianos gastan al año $21,1 billones en el consumo de cerveza," *La República*, July 4, 2015, http://www.larepublica.co/los-colombianos-gastan-al-año-211-billones-en-el-consumo-de-cerveza_272736.
6 Information received from Bavaria. Numbers from 2016.
7 Bavaria, *Informe III TRI 2014, Bavaria*, 2015, http://www.bavaria.co/docs/default-source/default-document-library/informe-bavaria-iii-tri-2014.pdf?sfvrsn=0.

8 Bavaria, "Informe a la Asamblea General Ordinaria de Accionistas sobre la gestión," *Bavaria*, 2015, http://www.bavaria.co/docs/default-source/default-document-library/informe-gestion-2015.pdf?sfvrsn=0.

9 Ibid.

10 All figures shown in the description of each World were obtained and calculated from Bavaria's 2014 and 2015 sustainability reports.

11 ISO 9001: Quality Management System; ISO 14001: Environmental Management System; OHSAS 18001: International occupational health and safety management system; ISO 22000: Food Safety Management.

12 According to Bavaria, the company pays 12 cents of a Colombia peso per cubic meter (m^3) supplied from surface water or rivers. This figure represents an approximate of 0.00004 cents of a US dollar per m^3.

13 $COP 10,605,815,192 converted to US dollars by using the foreign exchange rate of 3,149.47 COP per USD for December 31, 2015.

14 Bavaria, "Sigamos Prosperando: Informe de Desarrollo Sostenible— Resumen," *Bavaria*, 2016.

15 World Wildlife Fund, "WATER STEWARDSHIP: Perspectives on Business Risks and Responses to Water Challenges," *World Wildlife Fund*, 2013.

16 World Wildlife Fund, "WATER STEWARDSHIP STRATEGY FOR BAVARIA," *Technical Report—Step 4 Alliance between the actors for Collective Action*, 2014.

Chapter 9:   GRUPO HERDEZ TAKES THE INITIATIVE IN MEXICO'S FOOD MARKET

1 Grupo Herdez, http://grupoherdez.mx/conocenos/estrategia/.

2 Agreement issued by the Secretariat of Health with the guidelines for the producers of food and nonalcoholic beverages for the labeling and criteria for nutrimental distinctive, published in the Official Journal of the Federation, Mexico, April 15, 2014, http://www.cofepris.gob.mx/AS/Documents/Publicidad/LinEtiquetado.pdf.

3 Law of Organic Products published by the Mexican government (Congress of the Union).

4 IFOAM Organics International, "Principles of Organic Agriculture," IFOAM Organics International, http://www.ifoam.bio/sites/default/files/poa_english_web.pdf.

5 International Renewable Energy Agency, "A Renewable Energy Roadmap. Renewable Energy Prospects: Mexico," *REmap 2030*, May 2015.

6 Centro Mexicano para la Filantropía, "Informe Annual," *Centro Mexicano para la Filantropía*, 2015, http://www.cemefi.org/informes/informe2016/index.html.

7 Information provided by the Investors Relations and Sustainability Department, Grupo Herdez, 2016.

8 Global Reporting Initiative, "G4 Sustainability Reporting Guidelines Reporting Principles and Standards Disclosures," *Global Reporting Initiative*, https://www.globalreporting.org/resourcelibrary/GRIG4-Part1-Reporting-Principles-and-Standard-Disclosures.pdf.

9 Grupo Herdez, "Informe Anual Integrado. Financiero y de Sustentabilidad," *Grupo Herdez*, 2015.

10 Information provided by the Investors Relations and Sustainability Department, Grupo Herdez, 2016.

11 Ibid.

Chapter 10:   CHILE'S LAS PALMAS AVOCADO ORCHARD: WATER CONSUMPTION REDUCTION IN AGRICULTURE

1 UN Water, "Water, Food and Energy," http://www.unwater.org/water-facts/water-food-and-energy/.

2 Information provided to the author by the company by e-mail February 1, 2016.

3 Oficina de Estudios y Políticas Agrarias. "Frutas frescas," https://www.odepa.gob.cl/rubros/frutas-frescas/.

4 Fresh Plaza, "Avocado market still growing, Holland plays big role in it," June 13, 2013, https://www.freshplaza.com/article/2110214/avocado-market-still-growing-holland-plays-big-role-in-it/.

5 Interview with the author.

6 Daniel C. Esty and Andrew S. Winston, *Green to Gold: How Smart Companies Use Environmental Strategy to Innovate, Create Value, and Build Competitive Advantage* (John Wiley & Sons, 2009).

Chapter 11:   MABESA: INCREASING GLOBAL COMPETITIVENESS WITH ECO-FRIENDLY DISPOSABLE PRODUCTS

1 Carlos Richer, "The Disposable Diaper Industry Source," Richer Investment Consulting Services, http://disposablediaper.net/.

2 The Forest Stewardship Council (FSC) is a nongovernmental international organization dedicated to promoting responsible management of the world's forests. FSC certification ensures that products come from responsibly managed forests that provide environmental, social and economic benefits.

3 Richard Halbinger-Carmona, interview by Margarita Heredia Soto.

4 Mabesa, Research & Development Department.

5 Information on the socioeconomic levels in Mexico is presented in Table 11.2.
6 Richard Halbinger-Carmona, interview by Margarita Heredia Soto.
7 Ibid.

Chapter 12: WATER USE EFFICIENCY INITIATIVES IN NESTLÉ'S VALUE CHAIN AND THE IMPLICATIONS OF THE COMPANY'S BUSINESS MODEL

1 See http://ceowatermandate.org/disclosure/.
2 Nestlé Corporation, "Nestlé in Society: Creating Shared Value and Meeting Our Commitments 2015," http://www.nestle.com/asset-library/documents/library/documents/corporate_social_responsibility/nestle-csv-full-report-2015-en.pdf.
3 Ryutaro Hashimoto, "Current Status and Future Trends in Freshwater Management," *International Review for Environmental Strategies* 3, no. 2 (2002): 222–39.
4 Pay Drechsel, Patrick Heffer, Hillel Magen, Robert Mikkelsen, and Dennis Wichelns, *Managing Water and Fertilizer for Sustainable Agricultural Intensification* (No. H046805) (International Water Management Institute, 2015).
5 David Tilman, Kenneth G. Cassman, Pamela A. Matson, Rosamond Naylor, and Stephen Polasky, "Agricultural Sustainability and Intensive Production Practices," *Nature* 418, no. 6898 (2002): 671–77.
6 Drechsel et al., *Managing Water and Fertilizer for Sustainable Agricultural Intensification.*
7 Gil Maria Campos Alabau, Katy A. Shaw, Macaulay Reardon Kenney, Sarah Kalloch, and Tamaryn Nelson, *The Challenge of Positive Water Balance for Multinational Corporations*, Course report (MIT Sloan School of Management, 2015).
8 Carlos Lopez-Morales and Faye Duchin, "Economic Implications of Policy Restrictions on Water Withdrawals on Surface and Underground Water Sources," *Economics Systems Research* Issue 2 (2014): 154–71.
9 CONOGUA (National Commission of Water) Report, Numeragua, 2014, retrieved August 10, 2015, http://www.conagua.gob.mx/CONAGUA07/Publicaciones/Publicaciones/Numeragua.pdf.
10 Nestlé Corporation, "Nestlé in Society."
11 Ibid.
12 Daniel C. Esty and Andrew S. Winston, *Green to Gold: How Smart Companies Use Environmental Strategy to Innovate, Create Value, and Build Competitive Advantage* (New Haven, CT: Yale University Press, 2006).
13 Alabau et al., *The Challenge of Positive Water Balance for Multinational Corporations.*
14 Nestlé Corporation, "Nestlé in Society."
15 Ibid.
16 Esty and Winston, *Green to Gold.*

INDEX

9 781783 089123